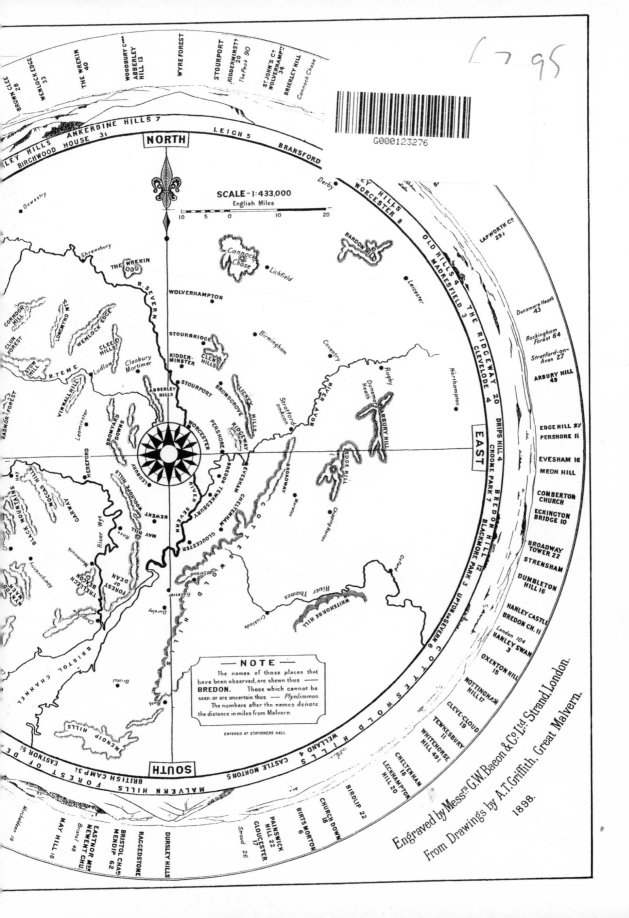

£7·95

G000123276

NORTH

SCALE – 1:433,000
English Miles

EAST

SOUTH

— NOTE —
The names of those places that
have been observed, are shewn thus ———
BREDON. Those which cannot be
seen, or are uncertain thus — *Plynlimmon.*
The numbers after the names denote
the distance in miles from Malvern.

ENTERED AT STATIONERS HALL

Engraved by Messrs G.W.Bacon & Co Ltd. Strand. London.

From Drawings by A.T.Griffith. Great Malvern.

1898.

The
MALVERNS

A 19th-century print of Malvern showing the south side of the Abbey Gateway and, to the right, Priessnitz House, which Dr. James Wilson opened as a hydropathic establishment in 1845. Much enlarged, it is now divided into apartments and known as Park View.

The
MALVERNS

Pamela Hurle

Phillimore

1992

Published by
PHILLIMORE & CO. LTD.
Shopwyke Hall, Chichester, Sussex.

ISBN 0 85033 819 0

Printed and bound in Great Britain by
BIDDLES LTD.
Guildford, Surrey

Contents

List of Illustrations

Frontispiece Malvern, 19th-century print

Introduction and Acknowledgements

This book differs from others I have written on the Malvern area because it is designed for use as a guide book by those unfamiliar with Malvern country and yet it contains material which I hope will be of interest to locals who have made encouraging comments on my earlier publications.

I would like to express particular thanks to Boehm of Malvern, Mr. K. Davis, Eastnor Castle Estate, the Elgar Birthplace Museum, Mr. J. Guise, Miss J. Hebden, the *Malvern Gazette and Ledbury Reporter,* Malvern Girls' College, the Malvern Hills Conservators, Malvern Hills District Council, the Morgan Motor Company, Mrs. F. S. Stewart and Bernard Thorpe who have lent pictures for this book.

The work of several photographers has been of especial value: Alix Gilmer took great trouble to produce specific views for me; Jerry Mullaney, who has for many years managed to produce the impossible, once more proved to be a friend to one in need; Mike Rowland kindly allowed me to select from his extensive portfolio, which includes numerous prize-winning pictures; Julian Salter also allowed me to use his work; and amongst the pictures loaned by the *Malvern Gazette and Ledbury Reporter* are several by their talented staff photographer, Sandra James (née Porter), whose early death saddened all who knew her.

My husband has also taken many of the pictures and has again supported me quite beyond the call of marital duty: his constructive criticism of my work is invaluable to me, even if my appreciation is not always immediately apparent to him at the point of delivery.

Pamela Hurle
March 1992

Chapter One

Malvern Landscape

Visitors to Malvern are usually impressed by the beauty of the hills and commons, particularly since most of the approach roads to the town are so picturesque; grazing sheep and ponies complete the romantic vision of peaceful rural calm.

Although the natural beauty of the scenery has provided a rare setting for the town, man has also had a significant part to play in making this area so beautiful. Given current concern about 'green' issues, the intervention of man may arouse suspicions about what has been done but, perhaps surprisingly, this intervention is generally acknowledged to have done much more good than harm.

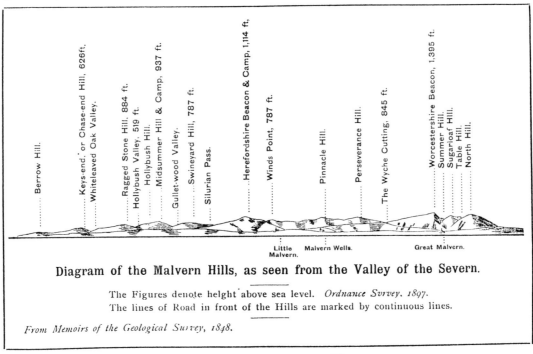

Diagram of the Malvern Hills, as seen from the Valley of the Severn.

The Figures denote height above sea level. *Ordnance Survey. 1897.*
The lines of Road in front of the Hills are marked by continuous lines.

From Memoirs of the Geological Survey, 1848.

1. Outline of the Malvern Hills.

One of the earliest examples of man's interference with the landscape dates back to *c.*400 B.C., more than four centuries before the Romans came to Britain, when an ancient British tribe, the Dobunni, were settled in this region. They built the prehistoric fort, British Camp, on the Herefordshire Beacon. This is the great hill (1,114 ft. high) towards the south of the Malvern range which, eight miles long, straddles the border between the old counties of Herefordshire and Worcestershire. Although the Worcestershire Beacon (1,395 ft.) is the highest point on the

1

2. Map of the Malvern area. Reproduced with permission.

Malverns, it is the Herefordshire Beacon which most impresses because of the ramparts and terraces which still stand as a tribute to the incredible effort and community spirit of those Iron Age settlers. More than 2,000 years of wind, rain, frost and sun have been unable to erode the achievement of sheer physical strength and determination, unaided by any earthmoving machinery that would now be considered necessary for such an undertaking. Another camp of more modest size was also constructed on Midsummer Hill at the southern end of the range. The ancient British settlers left the area at about the same time as the Romans came, though the theory that it was here that Caractacus made his valiant stand against the might of the Roman armies is now discredited. It had been popular legend in the 19th century and led Sir Edward Elgar, who rented a summer home in nearby Storridge, to name one of his most famous works after the hero whom he could imagine defending the great hill towards which he looked while composing.

The thousand years before the Norman conquest of 1066 were indeed the Dark Ages, for little is known about this region during that time. The landscape remained largely a wilderness. But the change of ruler, with the arrival in England of the

3. Birchwood Lodge, at Storridge, was used for several years as a summer home by Sir Edward Elgar, seen here standing outside the cottage. Over the years it has been extended and modernised, but would still be recognisable to him and his family.

robust figure of William the Conqueror made a lasting impression. Soon after he took control of England the new king decreed that great tracts of land should be designated royal forest, in which hunting was reserved for the exclusive enjoyment of himself and his favourites, though other individuals were granted various owner-ship rights. One such owner was the Bishop of Worcester, who was lord of hundreds of acres, but had to accept that the hunting and other rights he had once enjoyed over his land no longer belonged to him. One of King William's forests covered thousands of acres and at least 13 parishes – its precise boundaries are not now known – from the top of the Malvern Hills down to the River Severn. For long periods in the Middle Ages kings allowed favoured subjects to exercise the hunting rights, giving them the title Lord of the Chase. During such times the royal forest was officially called a chase, thus explaining the name by which it is still often known: Malvern Chase.

Whether it was a forest or a chase, the area was subject to a special code of laws framed to protect the deer and their environment. Anyone harming either the veni-son or the vert (the deer or the land on which they lived) faced fearful penalties. Local farmers, struggling to produce enough food to feed their families, were not even allowed to put up effective fences against the deer. If the wretched creatures trampled on or ate their crops they could do nothing except ask the forest officials to drive them off, being forbidden to do so themselves. Whatever the incon-veniences for medieval inhabitants, forest law had one long-lasting result for which we should be grateful. No one was allowed to clear land for farming or building unless they first obtained a licence. This was known as permission to assart and was not freely given. Since forest law was observed in Malvern Chase until the middle of the 17th century the development of the area was effectively frozen for nearly 600 years.

Events in our national history sometimes cause unexpected ripples or upheavals in local history. So it was that the financial difficulties of Charles I led to change in the landscape around Malvern. Locked in dispute with half of his subjects who were determined to limit his power and extend that of parliament, he cast around for sources of money without, of course, calling parliament. Hunting rights in a remote forest were of little use to him, but through a series of transactions they could be exchanged for what he most desperately needed – cash. He rescinded forest law, giv-ing up his hunting rights in Malvern Forest in return for a third of the common land, which he then sold. New farms were carved out of the land sold by the king, but local people were assured that they would not lose their grazing and other rights on the remaining two-thirds of the common, which would be left open and free in perpetuity.

Common land has for centuries played an important part in the economy of Eng-land. During the medieval period, when the population perhaps totalled about four million, parishes cultivated the most fertile land, leaving the poorer quality, the waste, for grazing sheep and other purposes. The waste was rough grassland, often with scrub or trees which might be a useful source of winter fuel, or food such as berries and nuts. It therefore added interest to a monotonous diet and helped to eke out a meagre budget. Over the years the medieval wasteland has become known as common land, leading many people to imagine that it was, and is, public land on which any individual might pitch his tent or park his car. This is not the case. The wasteland surrounding medieval parishes belonged to those parishes and was for the exclusive benefit of their inhabitants. So it was, in a sense, private property managed on behalf of the parish by the lord of the manor.

Naturally, then, there was much relief among local people when Charles I's disafforestation decree stated that two-thirds of the wasteland was to be left open 'for the freeholders and tenants and commoners to take their common of pasture and common of eastovers [right to windfall wood] therein as heretofore they have been accustomed'. But despite this guarantee, significant portions of the waste were lost during the 18th and 19th centuries. This was because of two practices: encroachment by individuals stealthily taking over common land adjoining their property, and enclosure of common land through Acts of Parliament. Enclosure, putting great tracts of former common land into private hands, made for more efficient and profitable farming, so was most popular with rich landlords keen to seize the opportunity to supply food to an increasing population. It enabled them to experiment with new crops and practise the new science of selective breeding in order to improve yields.

But many people saw enclosure as a kind of theft from the poor, who could not defend their interests against rich influential farmers:

> The law will punish man or woman
> Who steals a goose from off the common;
> But lets the greater felon loose,
> Who steals the common off the goose.

At the same time as increased anxiety was being expressed about the loss of common rights, Malvern was attracting large numbers of visitors for the water-cure, examined more closely in another chapter of this book. Local hoteliers added their voices to the clamour about the erosion of common land: since their livelihood depended on Malvern remaining an attractive area, they urged the recognition of its public amenity aspects, conveniently losing sight of the original purpose of common land. Some angered farmers by suggesting that cricket pitches and other features of interest should be provided for the visitors. The local press fanned the flames of the debate which raged for many years, and led directly to the most recent example of the way in which man's intervention has affected this area. In 1884 the first Malvern Hills Act was passed, setting up the Malvern Hills Conservators. This important local body was given the task of safeguarding the commons from further encroachment and enclosure, and the Act, passed at a time when public awareness was growing of the plight of the teeming masses in Britain's industrial regions, included a remarkably generous gesture. Focusing attention on the need for more state intervention to remedy the worst injustices and provide amenities which the individual could not provide for himself, reformers had already secured the creation of havens such as Epping Forest for the benefit of Londoners. Malvern's representatives sought to do their bit for the industrial Midlands – and for the local hoteliers -- by granting public access to the land put under the Conservators' control. At first this was a small acreage, but is now about three thousand acres.

This generosity made the task of the Conservators particularly difficult; reconciling the very different interests of local farmers with those of visitors has thrown up numerous problems, epitomised in the single word, dogs. Farmers with sheep on the hills have occasionally, quite legally, shot dogs for sheep-worrying. Dog owners have then become anxious about their pets', or even their own, safety. The Conservators have to sort things out. Their accumulated experience over a hundred years has taught them much which does not perhaps spring readily to the mind of the casual observer. For example, in exercising his grazing rights the farmer is actually helping the Conservators and visitors, for sheep make very good lawnmowers, reaching places that mechanical mowers cannot. It is the experience and care of the Conservators which keep the hills and commons of this area so attractive for visitors and locals alike.

The Conservators, who are unpaid, are locally elected and have complete control over a budget guaranteed to them out of local taxation. They also raise money from car parking fees and receive occasional grants from bodies such as English Nature to meet the cost of specific tasks. They meet every month to decide upon all matters of policy affecting the hills and commons under their control. Land acquisition, planting, provision of public facilities like car parks or cafés: these are all matters upon which they deliberate and decide. The actual work on the land is done by a paid workforce of about ten men who have considerable expertise and local knowledge. The vital link between the policy-making board and the men on the job is the chief ranger, who carries a heavy responsibility. There are also several paid and

4. The Malvern Hills Conservators have jurisdiction over the land through which run many of the approach roads into Malvern. The care which they exercise helps to create a favourable first impression with visitors to this outstandingly beautiful area.

5. Contrasting architectural styles in Malvern: (a) A Victorian house, built in Malvern stone before quarrying became controversial; (b) This picture of The Mount was taken in the early 20th century when it became part of Malvern Girls' College. Before then, it had been run as a girls' school by Rosa Burley, friend of Edward Elgar.

voluntary wardens. The characteristic which they all share is a great love of the hills.

Over the last 100 years, they have met some intractable problems. Of these the most significant was that of quarrying, which became a lucrative business in the early years of this century when the increasing popularity of the motor car led to a demand for improved road building. Malvern stone, lying under the surface of the hills, is a difficult material with which to work, since it fragments into irregularly shaped pieces. Buildings made from this stone require particularly skilled use of mortar, and are often dressed with other softer stone at door and window openings or corner angles. The town contains a good many Victorian houses constructed in this local stone, but demand for it was limited until the beginning of the 20th century, when crushed Malvern stone was found to be an excellent foundation for the new roads. Quarriers were able to make a good deal of money by meeting the demands of road builders throughout the country. Vast scoops were blasted out of the Malvern hills, causing unsightly scars, many of which can still be seen. The Malvern Hills Conservators, deeply concerned about what was happening, were aware that people were looking to them to stop the desecration of the area and endured the taunts of Bernard Shaw who suggested that the Malvern Hills looked set to become the Malvern Flats. In 1929 he wrote to *The Times*: 'In Malvern now the hosts of pneumatic drills never stop ... Day in day out, year in and year out, they grind and shriek and destroy ... The visitor ... finds Commerce, like Faith, removing mountains'.

6. Quarrying was a serious problem in the first part of the 20th century. The machinery and the work itself caused unsightly blots on the landscape.

7.   The ridge of the Malverns.

8.   Castlemorton Common, once part of the medieval Malvern Chase, is now under the jurisdiction of the Malvern Hills Conservators.

9. In places the Conservators have rehabilitated former quarry sites, as shown here at Hay Slad, where many people come to fill bottles with hill water: (a) the quarry; (b) in the 1980s.

The Conservators fought a long battle against the quarrying, but came up against the problem of the undoubted legal rights of the quarriers. Before the Conservators were established, local lords of manors had been fearful that any such body would deprive them of their traditional rights; they threatened to block the setting up of any board with jurisdiction over local common land. In order to overcome their opposition they were promised in the 1884 Malvern Hills Act that all their rights would be confirmed – including the right to dig stone, which at the time was no threat to the hills. When the motor car arrived, they found that they were sitting on very valuable stone quarrying rights, and the Conservators found that they had insufficient money to compensate them for the loss of those rights, even if they were able to secure the authority to do so. During the early years of the 20th century manorial lords began to lease out their rights to commercial quarriers whose activities soon led to unforeseen noise, some danger, unsightly buildings on the hills and costly damage to local roads as they carted stone to the railway stations in lorries with steel-rimmed wheels.

Repeated efforts, lasting some 20 years, eventually led to the Malvern Hills Act of 1924, empowering the Conservators to purchase those quarrying rights which were most threatening to the hills. Whilst this stopped further quarrying at Little Malvern and saved the skyline at North Hill, it increased the value of quarrying rights at other points on the hills. By the 1930s, when unemployment hit the country, the town was split into two camps: those who wanted to save the hills from further destruction and those who were more concerned about keeping quarrymen in work.

The bitterness of those years has largely been forgotten. The conflict over quarrying paled into insignificance when the world was plunged into the desperate conflict of the Second World War. When that ended, a good deal had changed and interest in Malvern stone was decidedly on the wane. Growing concern for the environment led the post-war government to designate Areas of Outstanding Natural Beauty, one of them being centred on the hills and commons under the jurisdiction of the Malvern Hills Conservators. The quarriers themselves were finding it more costly to extract stone -- in some places the water-table had been reached, so money had to be spent pumping out water which had flooded the bottom of the quarry. The combined interests of commerce and environment led to the closure of the last quarry on the Malverns in 1977 -- and hardly anybody noticed.

As the Conservators have taken control of former quarry sites they have rehabilitated them by landscaping and planting schemes. Some of them now have a particular appeal of their own: there is the rugged beauty of North Hill or the gentler aspect of the West of England site on Jubilee Drive. The pools which have filled with natural spring water at Earnslaw, below the Wyche Cutting, and the Gullet on Castlemorton Common, are very different from each other but they both retain the power to impress and surprise the visitor coming quite suddenly upon their deep waters surrounded by a towering rock face. These rocks are not for climbing – every year sees a crop of silly youths needing to be rescued by the long-suffering fire brigade – but to be enjoyed for their timeless beauty.

Chapter Two

The Priory

The centre of Malvern changed dramatically in the 19th century when the tiny village became a spa town, creating a demand for shops and other amenities. Until that time the focal point was the priory church, which now provides a haven from the bustle of the shoppers and traffic in Church Street. It remains one of the most beautiful parish churches in England, its history going back to the Norman period when it was built by monks who sought to withdraw from the temptations of the world and devote themselves entirely to the religious life.

This handful of brothers followed the Rule of St Benedict, who in the sixth century devised what he termed 'a little rule for beginners'. To most of us, seven church services a day and a good deal of hard work would appear more like an advanced course in the religious life, but Benedict lived at a time when masochists like the pillar saints and hermits went to extremes, competing with each other in feats of endurance to prove their faith; he wanted to make it possible for ordinary people to feel that they were devoting their lives to the God who was worshipped throughout western Europe in the rituals and ceremonies of the Roman Catholic church. A sound judge of character and perceptive about human behaviour, he pronounced idleness to be the enemy of the soul and set about ensuring that those who followed his Rule should have no time left to be tempted by the wiles of the devil. Every waking hour was occupied with prayer and work, including farming, preparing food and housework of all kinds. He also had the good sense to make provision for adequate sleep and a healthy diet of good plain food. Indeed, some might find his allowance of a pint of wine a day somewhat on the generous side. Malvern's small community of Benedictine monks, taking their three vows of poverty, chastity and obedience, never grew very large. Their modest settlement, however, grew from a typically Norman structure – notice the plain, robust pillars and rounded arches in the church – to a monastic complex dominated by a large and beautiful church embellished with late medieval Gothic additions.

A now discredited story about its foundation is that St Werstan fled from Deerhurst, 18 miles away, when early in the 11th century, he and other monks were threatened by invading Danes. Coming to the wilderness and presumed safety of Malvern, he set up a small religious community, only to be murdered – martyred for his faith – by another group of attackers coming from the west. This story was already regarded with some suspicion in the late Middle Ages, not least because no St Werstan appeared in any list of saints, but nevertheless is told in the stained glass in the north windows of the chancel. Such an origin would certainly have been financially advantageous to the monks of Malvern – money poured into Canterbury once its saint, Thomas Becket, had been martyred on the steps of his own cathedral's altar.

10. A view from Rosebank Gardens, showing the south side of the so-called Abbey Gateway and the tower of Great Malvern priory church.

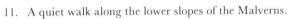

11. A quiet walk along the lower slopes of the Malverns.

12. The 99 steps lead from the left-hand side of the *Mount Pleasant Hotel* towards St Ann's Well. At the top of the steps Bello Sgardo was built in the 19th century on the site of St Michael's Hermitage, which is surrounded by legend. Werstan, once supposed to have been the founder of Malvern Priory, was said to have lived here. But was it, in fact, Aldwin? The original building was destroyed long ago.

The now more generally accepted story of the foundation of Malvern Priory is still not entirely clear, but a hermit named Aldwin seems to have come to Malvern Forest in retreat from the world. There was a small hermitage dedicated to St Michael on the hillside just below St Ann's Well, so he may have lived there for a time. With his companion, Guy, he planned to go off on pilgrimage to the Holy Land, in the tradition of the medieval Christian. Asking permission to do so from Wulstan, the saintly but eminently practical Bishop of Worcester, he was advised that it would be preferable to show his faith by staying in Malvern and founding a Benedictine community. His small band of brothers built on land belonging to Westminster Abbey, but remained under the supervision of the successive bishops of Worcester who, closer at hand, could exercise more effective control. The priory grew substantially during the next four centuries; although each individual monk took a vow of poverty, the community as a whole acquired more land and wealth from benefactors. This often happened in the heady religious atmosphere of the Middle Ages as men and women, anxious to buy what they may sometimes have felt was a rather uncertain passage to eternal bliss, bestowed gifts on monastic communities in return for the prayers of the monks and nuns inhabiting them. Visions of hellfire were a powerful incentive to generosity.

One of the most beautiful features of Malvern Priory is its stained glass, mostly dating from the 15th century. Medieval stained glass was produced for two quite distinct reasons: it was a means of worshipping the creator by furnishing his church with the best that craftsmen could produce, and it provided one of the earliest kinds of visual aid to teaching the uneducated some of the facts and beliefs then thought to be essential for the welfare of their souls. It is well worth using binoculars to see the detail in these lovely windows. A more modern piece of stained glass in the north wall, commemorating Queen Victoria's golden jubilee in 1887, includes a man rarely portrayed in England – the young German Crown Prince Wilhelm, later reviled during the First World War as 'Kaiser Bill', behind the queen, his grandmother.

13. North side of Malvern priory church from the churchyard. Charles Darwin's daughter lies buried under the tree to the left.

Malvern priory church also has exceptionally good medieval misericords or 'mercy seats' in the chancel, provided, as their name implies, out of pity for the monks who spent about five hours a day in church. In the normal sitting position they look like ordinary seats, but misericords can be tipped back, rather like a theatre seat, providing a ledge on which a monk could rest, taking the weight off his feet and yet still appearing to stand up. Many monastic churches had this type of seat, but few churches today can still boast examples so splendid as Malvern's, which show a variety of medieval scenes, with a particularly fine set of 10 which illustrate some of the agricultural labours of the time.

On the wall behind the main altar are over 1,100 encaustic tiles, presumed to have been produced in the medieval kilns which were discovered in 1832 outside the eastern end of the church. These tiles were the work of craftsmen, possibly from nearby Hanley Castle, where pottery was a thriving medieval business.

In the 1530s Henry VIII decided to do away with all the monastic establishments in the country. His new Church of England was almost identical to the Roman Catholic church in hierarchical structure, with the important difference that he, rather than the pope, was at the head of it. A prime consideration in his policy of dissolving the monsteries was, of course, the enormous wealth they had accumulated and which he could seize for himself. For Malvern the dissolution was particularly sad, for its monastic buildings, extended and embellished less than 50 years earlier, were in fine condition. Nevertheless, a king such as Henry VIII had to be obeyed so, soon after the dissolution order was issued, the sorry process began of pulling down the large complex of stone buildings in which the monks had lived, worked and worshipped. The working and living quarters were to the south of the church – the warmer side – on the site now largely occupied by the car-park of the *Abbey Hotel*. The valuable lead was being stripped from the roof of the monastic church when the villagers of the tiny parish had an idea which, like so many good ideas, seems with hindsight to have been the only sensible course of action. They had been struggling to keep in repair their parish church, dedicated to St Thomas and situated at the top of the village's main street, on the site where the post office now stands. As they compared their own dilapidated church with the fine specimen about to be demolished they reached the obvious conclusion, and the monks' church became their parish church purchased at a bargain price.

As the years wore on, the upkeep of so large a building became too much for the small community. By the end of the 18th century visitors criticised its poor condition: the exceptionally fine stained glass damaged by schoolboys throwing stones at it; the interior littered with rubbish and the droppings of the pigeons kept by the vicar in a loft attached to the Jesus chapel; worst of all, the poor state of the stonework which looked likely to collapse altogether.

It was the task of 19th-century vicars and congregations to save the building. Some of their efforts were seen as misguided: the architect Pugin was so incensed that, with more love of beauty than Christian charity, he opined that the building ought to fall upon 'and annihilate those whose duty it was to restore it'. Fortunately it did not. Later work in the 19th and 20th centuries ensured the preservation of the building for a good many years to come.

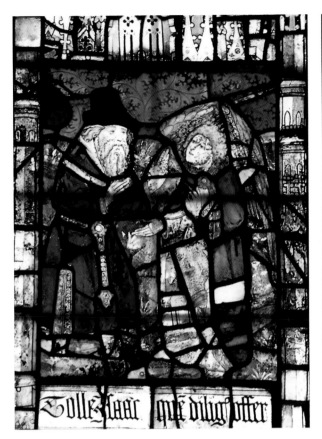

14. Over the centuries Great Malvern Priory's fine medieval stained glass was damaged, some lost, but its rare qualities are now recognised. During the Second World War it was removed and carefully protected in zinc-lined cases stored in three different places. It was replaced and re-dedicated on St Patrick's Day, 1946. This small sample shows part of the Old Testament stories portrayed in St Anne's chapel, at the south-east corner of the priory church.

(a) Abraham, in red, is told by a gold-winged angel to sacrifice his dearly loved son, Isaac.

(b) Moses forces Israelites to drink water mixed with the powdered remains of the golden calf that many had worshipped. If they were guilty of idolatry their beards turned gold and they were put to death, a fate being suffered by the unfortunate victim in the foreground.

15. Queen Victoria's Jubilee window is in marked contrast to the ancient stained glass.

16. Misericord seats in Great Malvern priory church show both the skill and the robust sense of humour of the medieval craftsmen who carved them: (a) A cat gets a taste of its own medicine as three rats hang it. Are they trying to teach the two owls a lesson about the fate that might befall those who snatch up living prey?; (b) One of the perennial labours – gardening under the watchful eyes of hungry birds; (c) This is probably a lion, carved by a craftsman who had heard of such a creature but never seen one.

The attractive churchyard has not been used for burials since the middle of the 19th century, when a cemetery was opened in Wilton Road, near Barnard's Green. One of the last burials in the churchyard was that of Charles Darwin's daughter, Anne, 'A dear and good child'. She had been sent to the healthy air of Malvern to recover from an illness but died there at the age of 10, causing great grief to her devoted parents.

The Benedictine priory dedicated to St Mary was so important to Malvern that it still dominated the centre of the parish in a map drawn as late as 1744. But today we have only two parts of it left: the monks' church is now the parish church and the gatehouse into the monastic estate now houses Malvern museum. The tiny rooms of the former gatehouse are now packed with fascinating pictures and objects ranging from medieval pottery to a rather frightening old drill used by a local dentist. Everybody calls the building the Abbey Gateway, but this is not strictly correct. Malvern Priory never attained the independent status of an abbey and the building, having several small rooms, was much more than a mere gateway. The little window through which the porter would check on any stranger seeking admission to the priory estate can still be seen. No one would be admitted, or allowed out, without good reason. St Benedict had quite a lot to say about the doorkeeper of a monastery: he should be a wise old man 'who shall know how to receive a reply and to return one', though he

17. Notice the old churchyard cross in this picture taken from the priory steps. It may be a 'palm cross' from the 13th century; during the Palm Sunday procession, consecrated bread and wine would rest on it.

might be permitted assistance from a younger brother – perhaps there is here an implication that the modern 'bouncer' has a longer pedigree than we may suppose. St Benedict strongly disapproved of monks wandering about outside, urging that water, mill, bakery and garden be provided within the precincts of the monastery.

18.   In the early 19th century Lady Lyttelton set up a Sunday school for 90 pupils in the priory churchyard. The Lyttelton school has been much altered over the years and is now the focus of the Well ecumenical project, designed to give practical as well as spiritual help to those in need. The school was closed in the 1940s.

Given his firm grasp of the realities of life, he was doubtless aware of the necessity of appointing a reliable doorkeeper who might judge how valid was the reason given by a persuasive monk seeking permission to leave the estate. Some of the ideas of St Benedict are part of the accumulated experience of every good parent or school teacher.

After the dissolution of the priory, local landowners took possession of the gatehouse and altered it from time to time. The most recent substantial alteration was in 1891, when the interior was totally changed and an extension was added to the west end. Its style is very different from that of the older part of the building, though the mock medieval battlement at the top of the north side mimicked the Gothic style. No sooner was it completed than a leading local figure, Dr. Charles Grindrod, condemned the whole as nothing short of 'vandalistic' – a strong word to use at that time. Oddly enough, though people today can readily spot the carbuncle added to one side of the building, they tend to be surprised that the battlement is so modern.

For much of the period since the dissolution the history of the gatehouse and the purposes to which it was put are far from clear. By the mid-19th century the upper

19.   Great Malvern priory church from the park.

20. Malvern museum occupies the gatehouse of the medieval priory. To the right of this picture is the squint through which the gatekeeper could see all visitors to the monastic estate: those who were unwelcome would not be allowed through the gates hung on the great posts in the centre.

floor was used as Malvern police court. The east side of the ground floor was used to store documents, whilst a shop selling fruit and game occupied the west side. In the early 20th century an old man recalled that in his younger days it was 'disfigured by a host of tin cats of all colours made for the purpose of scaring birds and on sale by the tenant of the Gateway, who raised vegetables on the adjoining garden'. By the late 19th century the gatehouse started to be used as offices by a succession of solicitors, architects and estate agents. One of these was Arthur Troyte Griffith, architect friend of Sir Edward Elgar, who named one of his Enigma Variations in honour of him. In 1940 Griffith himself wrote one of the most useful surveys ever produced of the gatehouse.

Eventually the gatehouse came to be used as staff accommodation by the neighbouring *Abbey Hotel*. Traffic still passed through, though it was, at least in theory, supposed to observe a speed limit of four miles per hour. Occasional slight damage occurred, but in 1979 serious structural damage was caused by an ice-cream van which became lodged under the archway. At last the authorities recognised the threat to this important part of Malvern's heritage and all traffic through the

21. The priory gatehouse before and after the controversial restoration of 1891.

gateway was prohibited. The gatehouse was subsequently given by De Vere hotels, owners of the *Abbey Hotel*, to the Malvern Museum Society, which was experiencing difficulty in finding satisfactory premises to house its growing collection of exhibits. This was an extremely generous gift: the museum could not have hoped for a more suitable building, and the gatehouse is its best exhibit of all. But it has left the museum with sole responsibility for maintaining one of the most historically valuable buildings in Malvern – a very heavy financial burden for a charitable organisation run entirely by unpaid volunteers.

But there is nothing amateur about the museum, which has very effectively displayed a great deal in quite a limited space. Much of the history of Malvern comes alive when you go into the old gatehouse, which is open daily throughout the summer months.

Chapter Three

Malvern Spa

Whilst the medieval period contributed much to Malvern's history through the impact of the forest laws and of the priory, an entirely different natural feature was to have the next dramatic impact on its development: the springs of pure water running from the hills.

Malvern water had long been renowned for its unusual properties, though precisely what these properties were did not become clear until the middle of the 18th century. Various pieces of 17th-century doggerel indicate that Malvern water was sent all over the country. Probably this all came from the Holy Well, which is now classified as part of Malvern Wells, but at that time was still within the boundaries of the parish of Hanley Castle. Patients also came to the well, which was on the old, less than satisfactory road from Malvern to Ledbury. Some were clearly disappointed, as Great Malvern burial register refers in 1612 to three people who had come to the 'holeie well'. Just above the Holy Well was the so-called Eye Well, now silted up, whose waters were supposed to do wonders for afflictions of the eye. One young woman from Bewdley was apparently cured of the 'scrofulous ophthalmy' which had prevented her from opening her eyes -- a cure with the disconcerting bonus of enabling her to detect a flea in her bedclothes.

The locals did little to encourage visitors to come to Malvern. There were few lodging houses and the roads were as frequently impassable and neglected as the rest of the roads in England. Celia Fiennes (1662-1741), indefatigable traveller and diarist, commented that the Malvern Hills were like the Alps, with 'much wet, the roads deep and difficult'. Nevertheless, many people came in the hope of a cure and John Chambers wrote in the early 19th century that accommodation was so scarce that perfectly respectable persons had to stay in the workhouse. In 1757 Benjamin Stillingfleet visited Malvern. He was the scholar who, attending the earnest gathering of society ladies in his simple blue stockings, led to the widespread, slightly derogatory use of the term 'bluestocking' for a woman with intellectual pursuits. Stillingfleet complained that, having been at Malvern for 12 days, he had found it difficult to find a lodging: 'the place is so full, nor do I wonder at it, there being some instances of very extraordinary cures, in cases looked on as desperate, even by Dr. Wall, who first brought these waters into vogue'.

In the early 1750s, Dr. John Wall, talented Worcester physician, artist and businessman, had analysed Malvern water and found it to be exceptionally pure:

> The Malvern water, says Dr. John Wall,
> Is famed for containing just nothing at all.

Dr. Wall's work increased the popularity of the wells at Malvern, but they were not

22. The Holy Well, origin of Malvern's reputation as health-giving and believed to be capable of healing a wide variety of diseases. The 19th century saw a legal dispute over the ownership of water from this spring; by the early 20th century J. H. Cuff bottled and sold it all over the country. When Cuffs gave up their business the building, like others close to it, fell into disrepair. The new owner, Mr. John Parkes, painstakingly carried out extensive restoration, reopening the well-house in 1977.

capable of coping with the great influx of visitors which resulted. Something needed to be done, so Dr. Wall and a Mr. Dandridge were appointed as receivers for a sub-scription fund 'to make the springs at Malvern more commodious and extensively beneficial'. Malvern was about to make its first concession to the tourist industry.

In 1761 a 'new house', presumably the fruit of the subscription fund, was built, and various public figures including Lord Walpole 'complimented the company ... with a breakfast'. Later on, William Steers provided accommodation at nearby Rock House and the Wells House. The latter, extended and altered, is now known as the Wells House School – a preparatory school which built up a fine reputation from 1870 but, sadly, closed in 1991. There are plans to start an international music and language school there in 1992. Samuel Essington's hotel, also quite close to the Holy Well, was opened in the early 19th century, and at Christmas 1810 was said to have gooseberries in the garden measuring one and a half inches in length and an inch round. (Clearly this was a time of climatic extremes – or wishful thinking – since five years later, in the summer of 1815, a violent storm was said to have produced hailstones the size of walnuts!) On the turnpike road to Ledbury, opposite the *Essington*, stood the *Admiral Benbow*, named after the English admiral who died in 1702. The name was changed in the 19th century to the *Hornyold Arms*, in deference to the owners of much of the parish of Hanley Castle. This building, next to the modern filling station, is now divided into apartments. According to local folklore, the admiral kept a mistress at a nearby house called, like his ship, the Ruby. The house was rented in the 1820s to the blind classics scholar, Hugh Boyd: young Elizabeth Barrett, who later married Robert Browning, lived five miles away and often visited Boyd and his family at the Ruby, where she read Greek literature aloud to him and much enjoyed his guidance in her classical education.

In the centre of the village of Great Malvern, stood the Jacobean-style *Abbey House*, predecessor of the *Abbey Hotel*, offering what we might today regard as unusually energetic breakfast facilities:

> At ten o'clock every Wednesday, during the season, will be a public breakfast, at 1s. 6d. each person, at Dugard's Assembly Room, in Great Malvern, after which 'the Shepherd's Lottery' will be played here.
> Music will be in waiting, in order to perform, if the company shall be disposed for a dance.

Dugard's advertised its high-class clientele: its charges were certainly such as to put it out of the range of any but the well-to-do. John Chambers, writing in 1817, pointed out that the terms were 15s. a week, 'exclusive of tea, sugar, fire and candles'. Hot rolls, tea and chocolate cost 1s. 6d. per person; public breakfast and balls were available on Wednesdays and a 'card assembly' on Mondays.

Up on what is now known as Belle Vue Terrace, an annual venison feast was established at the *Crown Hotel* (now the site of Lloyds Bank) in 1760. The lettering on part of the buildings on Belle Vue Terrace still bears testimony to the size that the *Belle Vue Hotel* once was, and the *Mount Pleasant*, with its delightful restored orangery, also lays claim to a history going back to the 18th century, though it did not apparently start life as an hotel.

In 1810, on the Worcester road, at the top of the village, John Downs built the hotel which bore his name; he found business so good that he extended it within a few years. *Downs' Hotel* was eventually to become the *Foley Arms*, though for a brief period it incorporated into its name the *Royal Kent and Coburg Arms*. It still bears the coat of arms that proudly shows its connections with royal guests during the mid-19th century. Queen Victoria, however, never came to Malvern, except as a child in 1830, when she stayed for 10 weeks with her mother at a house known as Holly Mount, opposite the *Foley Arms*. Edward Foley, lord of the manor of Malvern in the early 19th century, had improved the top of the village where the turnpike road from Worcester to Ledbury passed through. He and the architect Deykes must be given the credit for the attractive classical-style buildings which still exist. Barclay's

23. There were many 19th-century cartoons on the water cure.

24. Water flowing from the Holy Well.

Bank now occupies the building designed as the Royal Library. Kept in the 1820s by John and Mary Southall (he was the priory church organist and she the author of a fascinating guide to Malvern), it offered a wide range of goods for visitors and locals alike. It also offered weekly boarding terms of two guineas per person. In May 1830 little Princess Victoria came with her mother to a bazaar at the Royal Library. The village was naturally very crowded for this occasion, and the road from Newland 'presented a continuous line of carriages of every description'.

So, even in the 18th century there were modest boarding houses and hotels both close to the Holy Well and in the centre of the village of Great Malvern. But the full commercial potential of Malvern water was not realised until the 1840s. In 1842 young Dr. James Wilson arrived, full of enthusiasm for the ideas of Vincent Priessnitz, whom he had visited at Graefenberg in Austrian Silesia. Priessnitz, who practised for about twenty years from 1816, extolled the virtues of water, to be used both internally and externally in the treatment of all kinds of disease. He reached his conclusions through a series of personal experiences which seem to mark him as somewhat accident-prone. At the age of 13 he sprained his wrist and found that an effective way to relieve the pain was to hold his arm under a water-pump. Since he could hardly stand at the pump indefinitely, he applied an *umschlag* or wet bandage, which reduced the inflammation. Some time later he crushed his thumb, used the same treatment and urged others who had sustained injury to do the same – with the added refinement of covering the wet bandage with a dry one. People seemed content to listen to the harmless advice of this young son of the local landowner. He developed his theory further when a horse he was holding galloped off down a hill and dragged the hapless Priessnitz with him: the cart which the horse was pulling ran over the 16-year-old and crushed three of his ribs. His 19th-century biographer wrote that, having torn off the bandages, ointment and plaster of the local doctor, he

applied his own *umschlag* successfully. He replaced his broken ribs too, after a singular fashion, by pressing his abdomen against the window sill with all his strength, and inflating the lungs so as to fill out the chest, and then applied the *umschlag* to this part.

His scorn for conventional doctors was confirmed in later life when his wife insisted on calling one to their only son. 'He killed the child with one dose. From that day to the day of his death Priessnitz never allowed a drug doctor to enter his house, excepting as a pupil or patient.'

Wilson went to see him, convinced of the validity of his claims for hydropathy, and recognised that Malvern and its water could make him the Priessnitz of an English Graefenberg. Renting rooms at the *Crown Hotel*, he made enough money in his first three years to pay for a purpose-built hydropathic establishment which he named after his mentor. Priessnitz House still exists; now known as Park View, because it overlooks Priory Park, it was divided into apartments some years ago, the contractors finding during the course of the work some of the original plumbing and tiling from Wilson's time.

Dr. James Manby Gully, after whom Manby Road, near Great Malvern station is named, arrived in Malvern a few months after Dr. Wilson. He and Wilson started in

25.   The Council House. Once the site of Dr. Gully's grand home, it became first a boys' preparatory school and then the heart of local administration.

a spirit of friendship and cooperation, both disenchanted with conventional medicine and keen to use Malvern for a new kind of medicine at a time when medical men with inquiring minds were investigating all sorts of theories – anaesthesia, bacteriology, antiseptics all made their tentative appearance in the middle of the 19th century. Sadly, Wilson and Gully fell out, possibly because each laid claim to responsibility for the remarkable success of the venture that transformed Malvern from a sleepy village into a fashionable spa town. Gully lived and worked in the Wells Road, in two houses that overlooked Priessnitz House. He, like Wilson, was soon able to expand and live on quite a grand scale; he and his sisters moved house, out of the Wells Road and into a large house, just below the town's main crossroads. This house was named The Priory. Many years later, after Gully's departure from Malvern and after the property had been used as a boys' preparatory school for some years, Malvern Urban District Council bought it, to provide what must surely be one of the most attractive administrative headquarters in the country. Since it also incorporates the local Registry Office, its aesthetic qualities and splendid situation are particularly appreciated by bridal parties, who can easily use the adjacent park, once Dr. Gully's garden, to take their photographs. Gully used the Wells Road premises solely for his hydropathic work once he had acquired The Priory. This enabled him to insist upon a most unusual arrangement by which male patients

26. The so-called Bridge of
Sighs, linking Dr. Gully's two
houses in which he kept male
and female patients apart –
some say to protect the ladies
from unwelcome gossip about
their medical condition.

were treated in one house quite separate from the female patients in the other; the
two houses were joined by a passageway nicknamed the bridge of sighs. For many
years, until recently, they were combined as the Tudor Hotel, being separated once
more in 1991, but this curious connecting bridge may still be seen from the Wells
Road, just past Warwick House.

Warwick House itself takes its name from George Warwick, who set up a linen-
drapers in modest premises in 1833. The success of the water-cure in attracting large
numbers of well-to-do visitors to Malvern helped this small enterprise over the years
to expand along the Wells Road until it was the biggest high-class department store
in the town. It was a shock and cause of great regret when financial problems led to

its sudden closure in January 1992. Malvern waits with interest while the future of this historic site is debated.

Affluent visitors usually came to Malvern for about a month, placing themselves in the care of Dr. Wilson, Dr. Gully or one of the other doctors who climbed upon the bandwagon of the water-cure. A typical day started at 6 a.m. when attendants arrived in the patient's room, bringing a wet sheet in a large tub. Bedclothes were stripped off and the patient was wrapped in the cold wet sheet before being 'packed' with blankets and an eiderdown. Within minutes, sleep usually overcame the steaming patient who was awakened an hour later for a shallow bath which involved cold water being poured over him or her. A brisk rub down with towels was followed by the patient getting dressed and going to walk on the hills, with the object of taking fresh air and fresh water from one of the several springs. St Ann's Well, being nearest to both Priessnitz and Tudor House, was especially popular. It seems at 7 a.m. to have been as crowded as a modern high street before Christmas, though the band that played at this early hour was a German one rather than the Salvation Army. Malvern residents were sometimes offended by the behaviour of certain groups at the well, and one correspondent wrote to the *Malvern Advertiser* in 1864 that 'decent people are ashamed to visit it lest their ears should be defiled by conversation and scenes not very edifying in their character'. After a simple breakfast, healthy exercise in the form of walking or riding was encouraged, and the doctor might prescribe one of the more advanced, and intimidating, forms of water treatment. The douche, involving pouring gallons of cold water on the patient from a considerable height, not surprisingly aroused especial anxiety, though its devotees had nothing but praise for it.

The main meal of the day, served in the early afternoon, was quite large, but the food was not the rich fare in which so many of the patients indulged at home. Alcohol was forbidden and even tea and coffee were suspect, being considered too stimulating. Dr. Wilson also forbade his patients to write letters after dinner, believing it irritated the stomach and sent the blood to the head. Afternoons were another opportunity for patients to amuse themselves, perhaps visiting the country homes and estates of the local gentry. Picnics seem to have become popular with some patients, though the locals may have been less enthusiastic; at least one group of visitors settled down to their tea with bread and butter after 'the kettles were quickly boiled at the neighbouring cottage'.

The water-cure was expensive, costing between four and five pounds per person for a week. Since at that time the average wage of a working man was just a few shillings – perhaps a tenth of the cost of a week at the water-cure – hydropathy was only for the wealthy. So why did such people see fit to part with considerable sums of money to be ordered about by doctors who subjected them to sometimes very unpleasant indignities? The answer is that these people felt very much better after a few weeks of the lifestyle imposed by the doctors, which is hardly surprising when one realises that they came from a social class which ate far too much unhealthy food and, waited upon by armies of servants, took far too little exercise. Of course they felt better after a month at Malvern and believed the doctors to be clever men. They were, indeed, but perhaps not in quite the sense that their clientele fondly

27. Saving Cecilia Hall in 1981: (a) it seemed something of an eyesore viewed from Church Street; (b) the interior after restoration.

believed. Even in the 18th century Benjamin Stillingfleet had recognised that fresh air and exercise had much to do with apparently miraculous cures: the 19th-century doctors had the wit to channel this theory into commercial success.

But hydropathy attracted criticism – not least from the founder of the British Medical Association, Sir Charles Hastings, who lived nearby. Born in 1794, at Ludlow, he achieved recognition and a very comfortable income as a doctor by the age of thirty-four. He helped to establish the sound reputation of the Infirmary which had been founded at Worcester in the 18th century, and was knighted by Queen Victoria in 1850. By the time Hastings retired from the infirmary he was so widely respected that he was presented with a 1,000 ounce silver piece, costing 600 guineas, a huge sum in Victorian England. For many years he lived in Malvern at Barnards Green House, conveniently situated, perhaps, for firing off salvoes against the water doctors whom he scorned. He died there in July 1866 shortly after the death of his much loved wife.

Despite such opposition, the shrewd business acumen of the water-cure doctors transformed not only their own fortunes but those of Malvern as well. The little village set about serving the visitors, and new building turned Malvern into a town. Church Street lost its cottage gardens and orchards and gained little shops, where visitors might buy souvenirs or even forbidden booty, like cream cakes. New roads were constructed, named after the great or the good, like Queen Victoria and her husband or the lady of the manor, Lady Emily Foley, née Lady Emily Graham, daughter of the Duke of Montrose. In some of these new roads, like Lansdowne Crescent, lodging-houses sprang up to serve the needs of visitors, brought in ever increasing numbers once the railway line was opened in the early 1860s.

Malvern was now competing with the old-established spa towns like Bath, though the special property of its water was its purity rather than the minerals to be found in it. The class of patient was comparable, however, and provision had to be made for entertainment. One of the earliest ventures was a small concert hall, built in the mid-1850s and named after the patron saint of music, Cecilia Hall. It still stands today, halfway down Church Street, behind the Oxfam shop, though its existence was threatened in the mid-1970s when it faced possible demolition. Modest in size, but most attractive, it was less frequently used once a larger hall became available in the late 19th century. Lack of demand for it as a concert hall led to the indignity of its being used as a piano warehouse for Oxley's music shop, which for many years occupied the site in front of it. Fortunately, when it was no longer needed for this purpose, the philistines who wanted to pull it down were outvoted. Cecilia Hall was refurbished and is now the venue for a dancing school and numerous other activities. One of the best ways of enjoying it is to go to one of the functions which are now regularly held there during the Malvern Festival, which takes place early each summer.

Another facility which was provided in the early 1860s was a good railway service, with a particularly well designed station at Great Malvern and a more modest affair at Malvern Link. Two further stations were built in Malvern Wells as the railway line was driven west to Ledbury and Hereford, but neither was so aesthetically pleasing as those at Great Malvern and Malvern Link. They were designed by the same

28. Great Malvern railway station is a listed Victorian building. This view is taken from the spot where Lady Emily Foley, who dominated the manor of Malvern from 1846 until her death in 1900, had her private waiting room on the Great Western line. There used to be a Midland line to the left, where bungalows now stand. The steeply pitched roof of Great Malvern primary school (opened as Mill Lane schools at about the same time as the station) is a further reminder of Victorian architectural designs for public buildings.

29. Horse chestnut leaves and conkers on the capital of a station pillar.

30. An unusual touch showing the attention paid to detail by architect E. W. Elmslie when he designed Great Malvern station. Such carvings of animals can be seen clambering over both the station and his *Imperial Hotel*, which is now the main building of Malvern Girls' College.

31. The main building of Malvern Girls'
College. Formerly the *Imperial Hotel*, it has
been extended since it was purchased
from its German proprietor in 1919. This
independent girls' boarding school,
founded in 1893 by two remarkably
determined and far-sighted spinsters,
Miss Poulton and Miss Greenslade, is one
of the finest in the country.

32. Gryphons on Malvern Girls' College
gateposts.

London architect, who subsequently came to live in Malvern. Elmslie's Great Malvern scheme incorporated a grand hotel, a large, solidly built house for the stationmaster and a bridge over the new road (Avenue Road) which had to be driven through fields to provide access to and from the station. The station itself is now a listed building, carefully restored after a disastrous fire in 1986, while the former *Imperial Hotel* now forms the main building of Malvern Girls' College.

It is well worth spending time examining the station, built in Malvern stone and embellished with unexpected touches like little carved dogs clambering over parts of the stonework. Inside, the flamboyantly painted capitals to the pillars supporting the roof are today exactly as they would have been in the high Victorian period when, in an art perfected at that time, the functional was made as ornate as possible; the pillars did double duty as drainpipes carrying water from the roof over the platform. Sadly the original clock-tower has disappeared in the mists of time, though there are plans to restore it. Outside the main entrance there has been an effort to replant the gardens to their original pleasing state and to renovate the attractive lamps mounted on massive stone pillars, similar to those at the front of

33. A view from the top floor of Malvern Girls' College showing two domes: nature made the dome-shaped hill and man made the college's sports dome opened by the Duke of Edinburgh in 1978.

the old *Imperial Hotel*. Naturally, since they are now privately owned, neither the former hotel nor the stationmaster's house is open to the public, but, even from the
outside, both are impressive structures, despite the sad wartime sacrifice of some of
their intricate wrought-ironwork, removed in the ill-fated campaign to turn domestic utensils and ornaments into guns and tanks.

At the station, Lady Foley's tea-rooms serve very good food, though not on the
grand scale of the former *Imperial Hotel*, and commemorate the 19th-century lady of
the manor who reputedly refused to travel through a railway tunnel from her home
at Stoke Edith on the other side of the hills. Instead, she came over by road by
carriage and would wait in her private waiting-room, furnished to her requirements,
for the train taking her eastwards, and so avoided mixing with the riff-raff who
might be using the third- class compartments. She died as the 20th century opened,
on 1 January 1900, ending over half a century of matriarchal government in
Malvern. To her last breath, her timing was impeccable.

Chapter Four

Life in Malvern

Tourism first hit Malvern long before it became a household word to describe the periodic descent of hundreds of visitors upon a native population. The 19th century termed them excursionists, who often arrived on the special trains laid on by the Great Western Railway and the Midland Railway – in pre-nationalisation days two separate companies ran trains into Malvern. Some businessmen saw the commercial potential but not all were as successful as the doctors and hotel-keepers of the middle years of the century. One such scheme was a spectacular failure – the Spa Concert Hall. Few people now realise that a large concert hall, capable of seating 2,600, was built near the Wyche Cutting, next to the Royal Well Brewery Company in the West Malvern Road. Opened in the early 1880s, the Spa Hall offered an art gallery and extensive pleasure grounds, complete with a grotto, fountains and croquet lawns. Jenny Lind, the 'Swedish Nightingale', made her last public appearance at this hall: she sang at a concert in aid of the Railway Servants' Benevolent Fund. Now, however, nothing remains of the hall except part of an entrance pillar. Built too far away from the town centre, and when the water-cure was already in decline, it soon fell victim to competition from the more conveniently situated Assembly Rooms opened in 1885.

These Assembly Rooms have been modified several times and form the nucleus of the present Winter Gardens and Festival Theatre complex overlooking Priory Park. Old prints show that the original building owed much to the ideas of Sir Joseph Paxton, who designed the Crystal Palace. Paxton, once employed as gardener to the Duke of Devonshire, was naturally well acquainted with the design of greenhouses, but his enthusiasm for a large glass building to house the Great Exhibition of 1851 did not meet with immediate or universal approval. Extensive glazing became popular, however, after the astonishing success of both the Crystal Palace and the Great Exhibition, which was safely opened by Queen Victoria in Hyde Park despite the gloomy forecasts of sceptics who predicted that the structure would collapse from vibrations caused by guns firing a salute!

Malvern's Assembly Rooms were, of course, on a much more modest scale, but nevertheless were impressive for a town of its size. Shops at the entrance provided a useful amenity for middle-class visitors with money to spend, whilst the seating capacity was much more in keeping with the town's needs than that of the 30-year-old Cecilia Hall.

For the next 40 years the Assembly Rooms were the focal point for entertainment in Malvern. In the late 1920s they were bought by Malvern Urban District Council, which modernised them in time for the first Malvern Festival in 1929 – hence the present name of the Festival Theatre. Since that time, improvements have taken place, the impact of architectural styles of the mid-20th century on a 19th-century structure being very obvious, once its history is known.

34. George Bernard Shaw at a pre-war Malvern Festival.

The Malvern Festival was the brainchild of Sir Barry Jackson, who had already
established the Birmingham Repertory Theatre. He determined to make Malvern
the venue for a festival to pay tribute to Bernard Shaw, then widely regarded as the
greatest living British dramatist. (He was born in 1856 in Dublin, which was then
firmly part of Britain, whatever its inhabitants may have preferred.)

The first festival was held in August 1929 with no plans to make it an annual
affair, but it made such a favourable impression that a festival was in fact held every
year until the Second World War broke out in 1939. As the years passed, the scope
was widened to include the works of other authors, such as James Bridie, and films
and morning lectures were added to the entertainment on offer. In 1933 Sunday
evening concerts were introduced, one of the conductors being Sir Edward Elgar, by
then a much respected old man who died only six months later. Many years later a
bust was put up in Priory Park in his memory, so both leading lights of the festivals
were honoured, Shaw having himself planted a mulberry tree on the occasion of his
80th birthday in 1936.

There was a kind of magic about these festivals of the 1930s. The Festival Theatre
was widely described as 'the theatre in a garden' and in the garden a band con-
stantly played a variety of light music. With the Malvern Hills as a glorious backcloth, the middle classes loved the idyllic setting and the opportunity to mingle with
the famous, like Bernard Shaw and Dame Laura Knight, or with the soon-to-be-
famous, like Stewart Granger. Some joined the Festival Club in order to discuss the

35. The bandstand is a reminder of the pre-war Malvern festivals. It was re-erected in Priory Park in the mid-1980s, the initialled bricks around its base being purchased by individuals in the final thrust to raise the necessary money. In the background is a rear view of the Winter Gardens, adjoining the theatre and cinema. This picture explains the description often used of the Festival Theatre in the 1930s – 'a theatre in the garden'.

36. Swan Pool and the wooden bridge.

ideas and performances which transformed Malvern for two, three or even four weeks each year. Humbler Malvern inhabitants turned out to watch their social superiors at play.

The final pre-war festival closed on 2 September 1939. The next day Britain was at war with Germany. The pleasures of Malvern Festival were over, apparently for good. A festival did, however, take place in 1949, when the theatre was extended and Bernard Shaw wrote *Buoyant Billions*, 'the best play I can do in my dotage'. But he himself did not attend, the old romance and excitement had gone and Shaw, for whom the festival had first been launched, died in 1950. No one was much interested in Malvern Festival any more.

Then, nearly 30 years later, there was another revival of the festival, much more successful than that of 1949. They have taken place every year since 1977, so the post-war festivals have been held for longer than the original ones. They also put greater emphasis on classical music. There have been periodic doubts about funding, as indeed there were before the war. There have also been complaints about the cost of some of the events. But the social chasm of the 1930s has disappeared. The exclusive pleasures of the comfortably cultured for whom festivals started were not enough for modern Malvern. A wide-ranging 'fringe' programme of entertainment has been added to the more ambitious dramatic and musical events. This multitude of activities now offers something for everyone: festivals were originally feast-days, and Malvern can now provide a feast of entertainment, with something to suit every palate and pocket.

Of course the festival takes place for only two weeks of the year. But during the rest of the year a variety of activities provides entertainment and interest for visitors and local people. Apart from professional and amateur dramatic and operatic productions, the Winter Gardens complex is used for regular antique and craft fairs and may be hired for various functions; several of the local independent schools, for example, choose to hire it for speech days. From time to time over the last 50 years its financial stability has been questioned, its policies discussed and its future debated amongst the population in general and the local newspaper columns in particular. In 1992 debate focuses on improvements necessary if the English String Orchestra makes its home in Malvern. Such a decision would much enhance Malvern's reputation in the musical world.

Even if visitors choose not to go to the theatre or adjoining cinema they may still enjoy Priory Park, where in 1984-85 the old bandstand has been reinstated in its pre-war position above the Swan Pool. The Splash leisure centre was built in the park in the late 1980s to provide better facilities than the old open-air swimming pool.

Most people would agree that in Malvern locals and visitors alike can count their many blessings, for it is a delightful place to live in or to visit, and provides excellent facilities. Everyone hopes not to need a hospital – but if one does, there can be none more pleasant than Malvern's, originally built and equipped in 1911 at the expense of one of the town's most generous inhabitants, Charles Dyson Perrins. Davenham, his house in Graham Road, became a residential home for the elderly after his death in 1958. One of Malvern's secondary schools, to which he contributed

37.   This bust of Sir Edward Elgar in Priory Park was the work of Hilary Carruthers and was erected in 1960.

38. Viewed from the front, in Graham Road, Malvern public library has changed little since this early 20th-century photograph was taken.

substantially, is named after him and is a lasting memorial to a man whose generosity has sometimes been overlooked. The local council so shamefully neglected Rose Bank, the house which he bought for use as a public amenity, that it was demolished; its grounds, however, remain as a quiet haven, next to the *Mount Pleasant Hotel*, though occasionally, when they become overgrown, one wonders if they will suffer a fate comparable with that of the house. Dyson Perrins also contributed to the well-stocked public library, opened in Graham Road in 1906, and situated on an attractive site donated by the lord of the manor, Sir Henry Foley Lambert Grey, who could have sold it as prime building land but chose not to do so. Malvern has been fortunate in its benefactors.

It is also well endowed with clubs for practically every kind of activity, for Malvern's population is remarkably active, despite its (not entirely accurate!) reputation for being retired and elderly. This reputation is something of a hangover from the gentility of previous generations. The Second World War, and in particular the requisitioning of Malvern College in 1942, changed all this. Many of the locals feared that the young men and women who had come among them to develop vital technology for the defeat of Hitler would make Malvern, hitherto a relatively safe area, a target for German bombs. They hoped that, when the war was over, Malvern College would be restored to the boys and staff who had been packed off to Harrow, and the scientists would go away, leaving Malvern to return to its tranquil life. In fact, though no one realised it at the time, the newcomers were here to stay. The college returned in 1946, but the scientists stayed at establishments set up elsewhere in Malvern and have contributed even more to the continuing economic viability of the town than the water-cure doctors who had come exactly a hundred years before them.

Their contribution was not only economic, though the scientific establishment currently known as the Defence Research Agency remains the biggest employer in the town, notwithstanding numerous administrative changes particularly during the last 20 years. It employs articulate men and women who demand high standards – for example, the state schools in Malvern are among the best in the country – and have contributed a great deal to the social and cultural life of the area.

The story of the Piers Plowman Club has much to tell us about the wartime scientists and about society now, as well as in the medieval period and the extraordinary years of the Second World War. Piers Plowman was originally the subject of a long poem written in the 14th century by William Langland. There has been considerable speculation about Langland, some people believing he was born locally while others think that he was a Shropshire lad who came to Worcestershire, possibly to be educated at Little Malvern priory. He lived at a time when many people were disillusioned with the Church, which wielded enormous influence over the life of every individual and yet was riddled with hypocritical friars, greedy monks and lazy priests, and presided over by a politically motivated pope. Langland tried to put his thoughts and concerns about the Church and society into his allegorical poem, *The*

39. Malvern College, founded in 1865, was one of the new wave of boys' public schools. Designed by Charles Hansom (the chapel to the left designed by Sir Arthur Bloomfield), its buildings were requisitioned in 1942 for use by scientists. When the war was over the college returned from its four-year exile at Harrow and the scientists, at first so unpopular with the locals, moved half a mile away and became the backbone of Malvern's economic revival.

Vision of Piers Plowman. It is possible that this was written as he looked over Malvern country and saw how the beauty of nature was tarnished by the vices of humanity. Six hundred years later, when the world was torn apart by Hitler's war, many people in Britain were required, even if they were not in the armed forces, to work in places where they had no friends and where they were not welcome. Such workers were very much thrown upon themselves for entertainment and tended to club together. The displaced workers in Malvern called their club by the name of the legendary hero, Piers Plowman, and organised it to provide themselves with a few home comforts. As time went on, the club began to include lecture and drama groups, chess, bridge and table tennis clubs, community work and numerous other activities

40.   The 19th-century enclosure of Hanley Castle, Welland and other villages of Malvern Chase altered the distant landscape just as 19th- and 20th-century building has filled in the foreground of this view from the lower slopes of the Malverns.

41. On the West Malvern Road. In the background is one of the Victorian gas-lamps of which Malvernians are so proud.

so that it had in effect given birth to many clubs serving different interests. After the War, the scientists in Malvern were no longer lodgers but a new generation for whom Malvern was home. The Piers Plowman Club now had little to offer, as people could join a club which catered for their particular interest. The declining club was finally disbanded in the late 1970s. Some of the road names of Malvern, however – such as Bawdsey Avenue, Matravers Road, Orford Way and Steamer Point – are a permanent reminder of 1942's influx of workers: they are the names of places where the scientists of the Telecommunications Research Establishment had formerly been based. It had been moved about so frequently that one member of the team wrily remarked that he assumed that T.R.E., the initials by which it was habitually called, must stand for Touring Round England.

Malvern has retained a large degree of individuality and you will find few chain-stores here. There is a wide variety of small privately owned shops whose proprietors are keen to ensure that their customers are satisfied. Changes made in the rating system during the period of the ill-fated poll tax caused insurmountable difficulties for some and there were comments that the town looked like becoming nothing but a colony of building societies and estate agents. This trend has now been reversed. In the 1970s an open-air market was started in the Edith Walk car-park behind

Church Street – a revival of a 19th-century idea. On Fridays the centre of Malvern is always packed with shoppers, clutching vast bags of fresh produce, clothes and household necessities. The market became a tradition remarkably quickly, and a suggestion that, in order to overcome parking problems, the market should be moved to Saturday, was promptly squashed by a population well able to make its views known. The local newspaper, *The Malvern Gazette and Ledbury Reporter*, conducted a poll and no more was heard of the idea. This newspaper, which started life in 1855 as *The Malvern Advertiser*, has maintained a responsible and informative standard of report and comment on the affairs of Malvern, Ledbury and the surrounding area. For this we may thank three editors who over the last 40 years have been sticklers for high standards: Joyce King, who is commemorated in the wrought-iron gates at St Ann's Well, Edward Leigh Spencer and the present editor, Liz Griffin.

Chapter Five

Little Malvern

Little Malvern was once deep in the medieval chase, overlooked by the Hereford-
shire Beacon, beyond which lay the chase of the bishops of Hereford. The end of
the 13th century saw a bitter quarrel between the fiery Gilbert de Clare, lord of
Malvern Chase, and Thomas de Cantilupe, then Bishop of Hereford, over the precise boundaries between their playgrounds. The matter was resolved, and Gilbert de
Clare ordered a trench to be dug along the crest of the hills to define the boundary.
The remains of this trench are still visible today and are known as 'Red Earl's Dyke'.
The Bishop of Worcester also poked an irate finger into this quarrel: he actually
owned the land on the Worcestershire side of the hills and had to be placated since
his permission had not been granted for the digging of the ditch. De Clare agreed
to give him annually two bucks and two does in acknowledgement of his ownership.

Little Malvern, or Malvern Parva as it was formerly known, was like Great Malvern
(Malvern Magna) in the wilderness, thus offering seclusion from the temptations of
the world for those seeking the religious life. Another small Benedictine priory,
dependent on Worcester, was founded here in the 12th century but never attained
the size even of Great Malvern. It seems to have been viewed by Worcester as a useful detention centre to which troublemakers could be sent. A certain John de Dum-
bleton, for example, became prior of Little Malvern in 1299 but disliked it so much
that he asked to return to Worcester. The monks at Worcester, knowing that he was
a disruptive influence, feared for the safety of their eternal souls and made an abject
plea that they should not be required to take him back: 'we reverently fall at your
fatherly feet, and with heartfelt sobs we pour out our earnest prayers'. Eventually
the quarrelsome John went elsewhere, probably to Oxford where the infant university would have been better able to cope with a man of his academic leaning.

There is a local legend based on the misdeeds of a monk from Little Malvern
Priory, but although rumour has it that the legend is very old, it probably originated
only in the 19th century, when Charles Grindrod wrote his *Story of the Ragged Stone*. A
young monk was supposed to have broken his vow of chastity, having a love affair
with a local girl, later called 'the white witch of Welland'. His prior, on hearing of
the affair, ordered him to crawl daily on his knees up the nearby Raggedstone Hill
to atone for his sin. After performing this feat several times, the young man finally
in desperation cursed all upon whom its strange-shaped shadow, resembling a
cowled monk, should fall. By way of 'proof' of the effectiveness of this curse, we are
invited to note that the shadow fell on Thomas Becket, who met a particularly gory
death, and William Huskisson, mown down at the opening of the Liverpool-
Manchester railway in 1830 – the first fatality in a passenger railway accident.

By the early 14th century the monks at Little Malvern were rebuked by their
bishop for declining standards of behaviour, not an uncommon state of affairs in

religious houses once the initial fervour had worn off. The comments of Bishop Alcock in 1480, however, give more specific evidence of the type of behaviour which led to widespread criticism of churchmen and provided a climate of opinion which was to facilitate Henry VIII's dissolution of the monasteries half a century later. Alcock condemned 'the myslyvyng and dissolute governance of the bretheryn' who had 'byn vagabunde and lyved lyck laymen, to the pernicious example of all cristen men'. This was, he wrote, 'knowen through all my diocyse, to the grete displeasure of Godd and slaunder to the religion of the blessed Patrone thereof Saynt Bennet'. The ruinous state of the priory and its property was due, he went on, to the fact that 'Godd withdrew His grace and benefytes, and for the mysgyding thereof was not pleased'. After a couple of years in 'worshippfull and holye places' the monks, except for a certain John Wittesham who 'by the law may not be thear' (whatever had he done?), were allowed back to the buildings which Alcock had repaired. There were strict instructions that 'none of the bretheryn go into the towne or the fieldes without an urgent cause, licence asked and obteigned of the prior' and even then, no-one was allowed out without having 'a felow with him'. If the monks were disobedient they might expect 'grevous punyshment' but if they behaved themselves they were assured of 'Godd's blessing and myne'. Here, in Alcock, we see personified St Benedict's ideal for the monks to be governed by a father figure, capable of taking responsibility and exercising discipline over those in his charge.

42.   The east end of Little Malvern priory church, with historic Little Malvern Court to the left.

Little Malvern was one of the first monasteries to be closed by Henry VIII, in 1536, and was soon largely demolished, leaving only the eastern end of the monks' church which has ever since done duty as the parish church dedicated to St Giles. Even this small structure has at times proved too much for the tiny parish to maintain. In 1662, after the Civil War had been responsible for wholesale damage to churches throughout the area, the churchwardens reported the church out of repair 'in regard of the late warrs which did so impoverish the people that they were not able to repayre it, being known to be a very small and poore place'. The minister was a man of 'good life and conversation' and the parish clearly considered itself fortunate to have obtained his services, since it was the duty of the lord of the manor to pay him only a pittance of 'five pounds a yeare'. Things would have been little better by the time of Bishop Hurd's survey in the early 19th century, when the stipend of the perpetual curate had gone up to seven pounds, but Queen Anne's Bounty, a scheme devised to help in such dire circumstances as those prevailing at Little Malvern, enabled the income to be augmented by a substantial £200 per annum. For this the minister was required to take a service, usually Evensong, once a fortnight and should have taken a Holy Communion service once a year, 'but of late years there has been no communicant'. This was, of course, the period when slackness in the Church of England encouraged nonconformity to flourish.

Thirty-seven families lived in the parish in the reign of Elizabeth I; John Russell, a younger son of the influential Russell family from nearby Strensham, headed the leading family which was granted the monastic property and the right of advowson, presenting a curate to the parish. The Russells and Beringtons (into whom Elizabeth Russell married) have owned the Little Malvern property for well over 400 years, living in Little Malvern Court. This, being on the southern side of the church, occupies part of the site of the monastic living quarters, probably the prior's lodging. It incorporates some medieval buildings, including fragments of those parts of the church which were demolished. The family itself stoutly retained its Roman Catholic faith, despite all the penalties for doing so, and held services in their home. Once it became possible for Catholics to practise their faith openly, several churches were built in this area, which had always kept a strong allegiance to the pope. The wealthy Hornyolds of nearby Hanley Castle were also Roman Catholics and pumped money into numerous churches, including the grand church designed by Hansom for Hanley Swan, a more modest one in Upton-upon-Severn, and St Joseph's in Newtown Road, near Link Top. In central Malvern St Edmund's, established in the late 19th century, had a small community of monks attached to it, living on the spot where once Dr. Grindrod had kept his hydropathic establishment, Townsend House. Little Malvern acquired a Roman Catholic church, built by subscription, in 1862 and it is in the graveyard there that Sir Edward Elgar was buried in 1934, beside his wife, who had died in 1920.

Little Malvern also has strong connections with another leading figure from the musical world. Jenny Lind, Madame Otto Goldschmidt, came to live at Wynd's Point in the early 1880s, dying there, aged 67, at 5 a.m. on Wednesday 2 November 1887. She is buried in Great Malvern cemetery at Wilton Road: if you go in by the Wilton Road entrance and walk a few yards along the main path towards the chapel, her

43. A bronze statue of Bishop John Alcock, commissioned and given by Mr. and Mrs. T. M. Berington to mark the 500th anniversary of Alcock's restoration of Little Malvern Priory in 1482.

grave is on the right. Her funeral cortège of open hearse, coaches and carriages wended its way down through Little Malvern and the Wells Road to Great Malvern priory church which was filled to overflowing, a sea of spectators filling the churchyard. Amongst the many wreaths was one from Queen Victoria. Wynd's Point is not normally open to the public, but occasionally its owners, the Cadbury Trust, open the grounds in aid of charity.

Close to Little Malvern Court and Wynd's Point is the reservoir, opened in 1895 by the Duchess of Teck, mother of the future Queen Mary. It was an extraordinary feature of 19th-century life that, despite the fame of the pure water pouring from springs on the Malvern Hills, the vast majority of the area's population experienced difficulty in getting a supply adequate even for their demands, which today would be considered extremely modest.

Soon after this, Little Malvern became an area where quarrying caused particular concern. Since the parish was largely under the control of Charles Berington, who had rightly claimed to have done all he could to preserve the beauty of the hills, it had never been part of the area which came under the jurisdiction of the Malvern Hill Conservators. Some of his successors, however, leased their mineral rights to commercial quarriers and were at the centre of the battle fought against quarrying by the Conservators. Tractors and trailers rumbled from Little Malvern to the railway station at Malvern Wells, carrying tons of stone; they angered all who lived or worked along the route, not least because their wheels cut through the road surfaces which needed constant and expensive repair. Although quarrying provided a useful supply of jobs for local men, opposition to it grew more vocal: the blasting with its attendant noise and danger, the expense to the ratepayers and the disfigurement of the hills were all particularly acute at Little Malvern, where eventually the Conservators obtained the right to buy out the mineral rights, thus ending the quarrying in 1930.

Although there is nothing today to mark the spots of interest, two finds in the parish of Little Malvern are worthy of note, shedding a little light on the Iron Age community which lived in this region 2,000 years ago. The first was made in 1650 by Thomas Tayler, who lived so near British Camp as to be, as Dr. Nash the county historian vividly put it, 'within the distance of a musket shot of the trenches' of the hill fort. It was a gold coronet or bracelet, set with precious stones. The delighted Tayler sold it to a Gloucester goldsmith for £37. One wonders if he ever found out that the goldsmith sold it for £250 to a London jeweller, who sold the stones alone for the vast fortune of £1,500. The other find was made in 1847, when a family out walking found two pots full of brass coins dating from the third or fourth century. Unfortunately, in those casual days, people came along and helped themselves to the coins, several posting them off to their friends and relations.

Just above Little Malvern Priory there stood, from the 1750s until the 1980s, a little toll-house, belonging to the Upton Turnpike Trust, which was set up by an Act of Parliament in 1752. This has now been re-erected at the Avoncroft Museum of Buildings, near Bromsgrove, a good example of the much greater care that is taken today to preserve relics of past history.

Below Little Malvern Priory is Assarts Road: there is little of interest here, but the name is full of meaning. Assarting was the term applied to forest clearance permitted by special licence from the king or lord of the chase in the medieval period. In 1189 and 1196 the Bishop of Worcester was allowed to clear 300 acres 'neare the Bishoppe's myll of Wenlonde'. 'Wenlonde' was the original name of Welland and although the mill was destroyed in the 18th century the fieldname 'Mill Meadow' still exists. It is to be hoped that no-one decides to change the name of Assarts Road – nearby Sarts Farm was renamed in the 19th century and thus a little bit of history was lost.

Chapter Six

Malvern Link

Malvern Link tends to get overlooked or classed as a kind of suburb of Great Malvern, but in fact it holds considerable interest for those who care to explore. It was actually part of the medieval parish of Leigh, not Malvern; an ecclesiastical parish of Malvern Link was carved out in 1846, when the church dedicated to St Matthias was built, and the civil parish was the result of the Local Government Act of 1894.

There is a myth that 'Link' comes from the fact that horses were changed here in coaching days. This picturesque notion does not stand up to closer investigation as 'La Linke' in Leigh is mentioned in Pershore Abbey deeds of the 13th century, Leigh being part of that rich abbey's vast estate and within the medieval administrative area known as Pershore Hundred. It probably derives from the Old English word, *hlinc*, meaning gently sloping ground, which is certainly an apt description of the present Link common, the manicured relic of Malvern Chase. Malvern Chase was under the overall authority of the Chief Forester at Hanley Castle but he was assisted by subordinate foresters who were responsible, rather like policemen on their beat, for parts of the forest known as walks. The keeper of the Link Walk is reputed to have lived in Beauchamp Cottage, the attractive little black and white cottage at the junction of Pickersleigh Avenue and Worcester Road. An ancient stone, believed to mark the boundary between Leigh and Powick, was mentioned in a perambulation of Malvern Chase recorded in 1584: the forest keeper, Buckwell, 'brought us unto a great stone in a tufte of bushes and said "here endethe my walk of the linke and Clifhey wode"'. This stone is probably the one marked on the Foley estate map drawn by John Doharty in 1744 and is now in the churchyard of St Matthias.

Whilst tracing medieval ownership of the manor of Leigh makes dull reading, it is worth noting that by the 18th century it had passed into the hands of the Cocks family, who later built Eastnor Castle. This connection with the Somers-Cocks family, which sold some 70 acres in the mid-19th century, explains road names such as Somers Park Avenue, a quite ordinary residential area with a primary school now its focal point.

Leigh made a little legal history in being the first of the parishes of the medieval chase to enclose its common land. In the villages which had comprised Malvern Chase the notion of enclosure led to heated arguments, as there were particular features of the medieval chase which made enclosure even more difficult than usual. Whilst it was usual for common rights on wasteland to belong exclusively to the particular parish in which the wasteland was situated, in the chase there had been intercommoning, allowing all the chase parishes to 'pool' their wasteland. The announcement that Leigh was to enclose caused consternation in the other 12

44. The Link Stone, in the churchyard of St Matthias' church, may have been a hoar stone or boundary mark in its original position. Coins are said to have been placed in such stones by travellers crossing the parish boundary – one wonders how long they were left there!

parishes of the former chase. It therefore took a considerable time to carry out the terms of the Enclosure Act passed in 1776, and the dust did not settle for a long time after that, even though there was an extensive tract of common land left. Indeed, there are stories that not only were the hated enclosure fences pulled up and burned, but that a whole family was murdered in their beds by the fence breakers, anxious to avoid being named to the authorities. Magistrates would have passed stiff sentences to make the offenders a public example and discourage others from interfering with the enclosing of the common, so those who destroyed the new fences in the parish of Leigh silenced forever the witnesses to their crime.

An important feature of the old parish of Leigh still stands half a mile west of the A4103 to remind us of both its agricultural past and of the immense wealth and power of the medieval church. This is the cruck-framed tithe barn, believed to be the largest in the world, where crops owed to Pershore Abbey were stored in medieval times, its size indicating just how rich the abbey was. The barn was recently restored under the auspices of English Heritage and is now open to the public in the summer months, though it remains in daily use as part of a working farm. Leigh

45.   Part of the roof of the huge tithe barn at Leigh, shown here before its restoration in the late 1980s.

manor and tithe barn passed into lay hands when Pershore Abbey's estates were dispersed. The abbey itself was partly destroyed, and the remnant of its church, like that at Little Malvern Priory, was turned to use as a parish church.

Some large houses overlooking the Link common, on the left-hand side of the road to Worcester, indicate that there was enough money in the upper part of Malvern Link to build in quite a grand style. Nevertheless, a map of 1831 clearly shows a workhouse, which must have lowered the tone, overlooking the common in the Worcester Road. Later on a tramps' ward was set up nearby and used to accommodate vagrants after Malvern became part of the Upton Poor Law Union, as a result of the far-reaching 1834 Poor Law Amendment Act. The Union workhouse was built in Upton in 1836, but not even the hard-boiled officials of the 19th-century poor law required vagrants to tramp seven miles to Upton to find a bed for the night.

The lower part of Malvern Link as we see it today is largely a 19th- and early 20th-century development, and many of its residents were regarded as socially inferior to the genteel inhabitants of Great Malvern. In her fascinating account of Malvern Link, Daphne Drake quotes Canon Newbolt, vicar of St Matthias in the 1880s: 'we sent up labourers, they sent down washing'.

Bringing the railway to Malvern Link in 1859 encouraged the growth of population. Soon a rather grand station was opened. This was designed by E. W. Elmslie and, like his station complex at Great Malvern, came complete with adjoining hotel. The hotel, a little like a modest château, did not prove very successful, and was turned into a school in the 1870s. It was pulled down in the 1960s – regarded by many as an act of wanton vandalism – and the site is now covered with modern apartments.

The station at the Link put an end to the old business of taking a coach. In the 18th century coaching had become popular, using the roads built by the proliferating turnpike trusts, and there was a toll-bar with turnpike cottage down in the Link and another just beyond Link Top, where Bank Street joins the Worcester Road. Even after railways began to criss-cross the land, visitors to Malvern could get no further than Worcester, where they would have to take a coach and drive through a fertile tract of countryside used for growing apples, pears, hops and grain. In 1856 one appreciative visitor described his journey towards Malvern, where

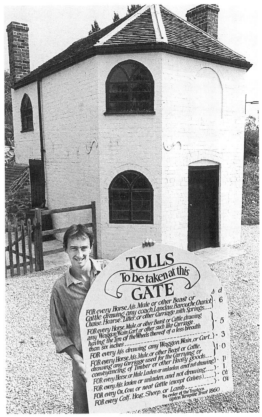

46. The old toll-house at Little Malvern was re-erected in the late 1980s at the Avoncroft Museum of Buildings, near Bromsgrove. It is shown here just before the table of tolls was affixed above the main door.

> the mountain chain rises ... ever higher and changes gradually from grey to green ... Then the white dwellings of Great Malvern sparkle in the warm light, and the square tower of the Priory Church peeps out among the trees; and anon we are rattling along the common and entering the town.

Delightful though this may sound, it is a romantic image of coach travel which was, in truth, uncomfortable and frequently dangerous. The coming of the railway made it much more realistic for people to work in Worcester or other towns and live in the Link, thereby encouraging the growth of population which is particularly apparent from this time. In the final decade of the 19th century a substantial property came up for sale and was transformed into a housing estate and block of shops just below the station. Redland Road and the anti-royalist sounding Cromwell and Hampden Roads now appeared, together with the Colston Buildings, originally

47.   The Santler Malvernia car in the summer of 1988. Owners Dr. and Mrs. Sutton stand each side of it.

planned as a unit but now rather spoilt by differing ground floor façades. A similar fate befell the Exchange Building by the traffic lights in Great Malvern.

Another dramatic change in transport occurred in the 20th century with the arrival of the motor car, and Malvern Link played an important part in the development of this new-fangled machine. Two separate manufacturers produced early cars. The Santler brothers designed experimental vehicles, at first using steam and gas and eventually producing a petrol driven car, still in existence, having been restored by its present owner. But their company ceased production in the 1920s and today few people, except vintage car specialists, have heard of the Santler Malvernia. The famous Morgan cars were originally produced in Malvern Link at the workshops behind the filling station currently trading as Brooklyn Garage. The company moved to a new site in the Pickersleigh Road in 1919 and, despite the efforts of high profile businessmen, has staunchly resisted the temptation to develop production line techniques, recognising that part of the appeal of a Morgan car is the individuality of a vehicle still largely produced by hand. Fewer than 10 are

48.   Infinite care goes into the production of each Morgan car at the factory in Malvern Link.

produced each week, so if you want one of these very special cars you can expect to wait years for it!

In the late 1830s the Nonconformists opened in the Link a chapel of the Countess of Huntingdon's Connexion. This was the heyday of the two religious societies which had been founded to educate poor children: the Church of England founded the National Society, whilst the Nonconformists had their British and Foreign Society. There was considerable rivalry between the two in the battle to win thousands of little hearts and minds to fill their respective churches. This battle seems to have been fought out in the Link, where a British School appeared behind the Countess of Huntingdon chapel and a National School opened in Upper Howsell soon after St Matthias' church was consecrated. Since education was still a privilege rather than a right, this also marks a genuine concern felt by men like the grocer and draper, Mr. Towndrow, who supported the Nonconformists, and by Lord Somers and the new incumbent at St Matthias'. One of the applicants for the post of schoolteacher at St Matthias' school, a young student, was described by her college principal as 'well-looking, but not handsome' – an irrelevant comment unlikely to find favour today! If such were the criteria applied in appointing staff it may help to explain the report in 1861 of the school inspectors that the school was feeble, the headmaster apparently lacking energy and skill. A new school, known as Malvern Link National School was opened in 1862, with new staff, on a half-acre site near the church.

St Matthias' church was built in typically Victorian Gothic style, on part of the old Link Meadow, the three-quarters of an acre site granted in 1843 by the lord of the manor of Leigh, Lord Somers. The small church at Leigh and a chapel at Bransford were too small and too far away to meet the needs of the growing community in the Link, and even the new church needed to be extended three times, in 1858, 1862 and 1880. The smaller congregations of the late 20th century have enabled the back of this very large church to be turned into a social centre, attracting new people into the fellowship of the church and coinciding with the decade of evangelism with which churches countrywide are closing this century.

At the end of the 19th century the Church of England experienced a revival of the fervour which it had so lamentably failed to possess in the early years of that century, and yet another church – the Church of Ascension – was built in 1903 at the top of Somers Park Avenue, according to the plans of a rising young architect, Mr. (later Sir) Walter Tapper. So many cottages had been built on the brickfields of Quest Hills Road and the pasture land at Link Top that it was named, rather derisively, Newtown. The nickname stuck.

It was Newtown that was favoured with Malvern's first hospital, opened in 1868 in a cul-de-sac unimaginatively called Hospital Bank, off Newtown Road. The building, another interesting piece of Malvern's Victorian Gothic architecture, is still there, though the hospital was replaced in the early years of the 20th century. Looking at the building, it is quite easy to imagine the regime which prevailed there – patients were even expected to help with washing and ironing the linen or cleaning the wards, if the doctor considered them fit enough!

Another sign of religious fervour was the establishment of a convent, the Community of the Holy Name, in Ranelagh Road, at the bottom of Malvern Link in

1887. A history of this community was published in 1950 and further information was devotedly recorded by one of its number, Sister Jane, who died shortly before its removal to Derby in 1990. The buildings are still there though a question mark hangs over their future. There are many people particularly concerned about the possible fate of the heart of the large complex of buildings, the chapel, designed by Sir John Ninian Comper. The community sent its younger members out as missionaries to Africa, but also did work at home for the young, the elderly and the sick. For some years it ran a home for women in the former St Edward's Orphanage in West Malvern Road. This well-run 19th-century foundation ceased to be an orphanage at the end of the Second World War and is now used as a Baptist Conference Centre. Its warden sees a wide spectrum of human emotions displayed by men returning to their childhood home and by the parents whose circumstances forced them to put their children there. The convent in the Link was regarded as home by the nuns who were sent further afield to do their work, and the community owned considerable property in the Ranelagh Road area. This included not only the extensive convent buildings but also the gardens used to produce their own food and the former Home of the Good Shepherd, which took in so-called 'fallen women'. Homes for fallen women ceased to be needed in a society which no longer stigmatised illegitimacy so it became St Michael's Nursing Home. Declining numbers of women prepared to take religious vows made it impracticable to maintain so large and rambling a complex of buildings and so the Link has lost the group which contributed so much to the area for over a century.

But in other ways life in the Link has become more bustling and full of activity. A light industrial estate has been established in Spring Lane; nowadays few people realise that all the cars, lorries and vans are travelling along the winding road that went past a natural spring now hidden from view by modern buildings. Further up, Tanhouse Lane reminds us of the importance of the leather industry in the medieval forest, but the tanners have been replaced by a new group of craftsmen producing a commodity which has delighted thousands for many years -- high quality hand-crafted porcelain. Boehm porcelain was first produced in the United States in the 1950s and the company expanded to Malvern in the early 1970s. Mrs. Helen Boehm has a reputation for her exuberance and charitable works; her workforce has a similarly enviable reputation for its high standards. Like Morgan cars and Malvern water, Boehm porcelain ensures that the name of Malvern is known throughout the world for the excellence and individuality of its products.

Chapter Seven

On the Hills

For thousands of people, walking on the Malvern Hills is a particular delight. Many have their own favourite spot and would not thank any author for divulging it to the world at large. But there are some places on the hills which should not be missed. This chapter aims to give some information about some of these popular parts, leaving you to find your own more private spots. Serious explorers would be well advised to buy a detailed map – there is a particularly useful set locally available which contains notes and comments on geology and places of interest.

The Malvern Hills Conservators have had to come to terms with the fact that thousands of people love the Herefordshire Beacon, with its ancient British hill-fort, so they have provided quite a large and convenient car-park at the bottom of it. More controversially, they have provided something which is rarely to be found on the hills – a tarmac path. This has angered many people, as it is clearly not a natural path. The critics, however, may not be aware that nature simply cannot cope with the number of walkers now arriving in their cars from all over the country. Years ago, nature could cope with a few hundred people regularly climbing the hill, especially since far fewer came in the winter months, giving the ground time to recover. Today, something like one million pairs of feet climb up that hill every year: the original path became so muddy and churned up that people walked to the side of it, eroding a very considerable area of land; more robust varieties of grass were sown (the purists complaining that this was not natural), but the problem remained, so wooden retaining planks were tried, achieving little more success. In desperation, the Conservators resorted to tarmac; it may not be universally popular, but it has undoubted advantages, enabling even the less agile to climb to the top of the hill as they dearly want to, and safeguarding land from erosion.

The British Camp car-park is at the side of the A449. Opposite the car-park is the *Malvern Hills Hotel*, still called by its old name, the *British Camp*, by the locals. Some of them may even use its 19th-century name – *Peter Pocket's*. Near here was the spot where, in the 17th century, Thomas Tayler found an ancient gold coronet set with jewels.

Near here the A449 meets the B4232, usually known as Jubilee Drive because it was built by public subscription in celebration of Queen Victoria's Golden Jubilee in 1887. There was some consternation about finding the final £214, for which a fund-raising three day bazaar was held in the Malvern Assembly Rooms in 1889. Although promoted by a stalwart champion of commoners' rights, Stephen Ballard, who contributed to it generously in a variety of ways, it was not an entirely popular scheme. Cutting through useful grazing land, it was resented by many locals who saw it as pandering to tourists whom they had no desire to encourage. It soon became extremely popular for drives, offering panoramic views over Herefordshire and beautiful scenery whatever the season. Quite alpine in both appearance and the demands it makes on a driver's concentration, it is definitely not to be taken at speed. A car-park at Black Hill, some yards beyond the *Malvern Hills Hotel*, provides the opportunity for an easy walk to the ridge of the hill from which there are good views across Worcestershire.

At its northern end, Jubilee Drive meets the old road known as the Wyche Cutting, a pass through the hills of comparable age to that at British Camp. Its name may derive from the fact that it was an old saltway, along which horses, mules or donkeys brought Droitwich salt into Herefordshire and the west. The route, going behind the *Herefordshire Inn*, was altered in 1836. After crossing this junction, the modern motorist might take the West Malvern Road, a continuation of the B4232. Along both Jubilee Drive and the West Malvern Road is plenty of evidence of the quarrying which threatened the Malverns before the Second World War. It is unwise, and at places illegal, to park on these roads, but there are parking areas which allow those who want to explore the hills on foot to leave the car. The people of West Malvern have their own village shops, services and church. Roget, who compiled the well-known *Thesaurus of English Words and Phrases*, enjoyed regular holidays in the Malverns. He died at West Malvern in 1869 and is buried in the churchyard. Nearby, there is a girls' boarding school, St James and the Abbey, in the former residence of Lady Howard de Walden. Her obituary in 1899 described her as perhaps the most eccentric woman in Britain and claimed that she owned more houses than anyone else in the world. She spent a vast fortune, about £100,000, on her West Malvern mansion and also gave about £4,000, a very generous sum for those days, to provide hill-paths on the Malverns.

At the Wyche Cutting you might choose to go along the eastern rather than the western side of the hills. If so, as you go through the Wyche Cutting you will immediately have a splendid view of the Worcestershire plain. A few yards down, on the left and just north of the Wyche Cutting, is the fascinating Earnslaw Pool. Once a quarry which caused subsidence problems at the ridge of the hill in the 1930s, this has now filled naturally with water, where fish have been bred in recent years. An idyllic spot, perfect for families, it enables toddlers to dabble their toes at the water's edge. This is perhaps a point at which to sound a note of warning: although the Malverns are a wonderful playground for young and old alike, it is not safe for children to be left unsupervised on them at any time. It is very easy to slip or even for the very young to get lost.

Between the Wyche Cutting and Earnslaw Pool there is a spot known as the Gold Mine, where several hill-paths meet. In the early 18th century a Bristol man, convinced that there were precious minerals to be found on the hills, spent a fortune sinking a shaft deep into the ground. Needless to say, he was as successful as those who believed that the streets of London were paved with gold.

The highest point on the Malverns, the Worcestershire Beacon, may be reached by several paths. It is well worth the effort of climbing to this historic spot, on which bonfires have been lit since time immemorial on occasions of national alarm or jubilation, from the threat of invasion to the celebration of a royal wedding. For Queen Victoria's Diamond Jubilee the bonfire was, according to the local press:

49.   This sentence in the stocks does not seem too painful!

the largest that has ever irradiated from Malvern's heights ... Its centre consisted of an iron pipe, 18 inches in diameter, stopped with concrete, round which 400 railway sleepers were stacked, held in position by iron ties. Between these there was stowed a quantity of miscellaneous combustibles. Besides the sleepers there were requisitioned: 20 scaffold poles, five tons of hop-poles, 30 tar barrels, a quantity of liquid and consolidated petroleum ... two loads of saw-mill waste, gorse, four tons of cordwood and 2,000 faggots.

It was a much more successful affair than the Golden Jubilee bonfire, which burned for weeks and destroyed everything in what one conservator lamented was a large 'stretch of charred surface'. More permanent a memorial than the Diamond Jubilee bonfire was the toposcope, designed by Arthur Troyte Griffith, though even the normally efficient Victorians failed to put it up on time. It was eventually unveiled in June 1899, on the 62nd anniversary of the Queen's accession, a day marred by rain, which led to a less dignified ceremony than the planners might have wished for. Since that time it has given pleasure to many, as they try to detect points of interest in the surrounding counties with the aid of the directions on its engraved plate.

The Worcestershire Beacon was a favourite spot with the Victorians, who loved to take a donkey ride to the top. These donkeys, like much else, disappeared when the Second World War started, but generations of them offered a welcome means for the frail or the lazy to enjoy the views without the trouble of using their own legs. Much 19th-century ink was devoted to writing about them, often with a subtle hint to visitors to try to safeguard them from the sticks and pins of the youngsters who were paid by their owners to escort them. The following extract is taken from *Leisure Hour* (1862):

> The Malvern donkeys are certainly thwacked more than is needful, and I am not without my suspicions of pins being somewhat too freely used in connection with the extremities of the donkey and the driver's stick; but ... these donkeys are well cared for ... The donkeys are stabled during the night, and have a mouthful of hay; during the day they receive three feeds of oats, beans, bran and chaff; and after every journey they are indulged with a complementary feed. On their way down from the hill-top they can also snatch a few minutes' browse on ferns and thymy grass ... Thus they are not stinted on their food and the mediation of their tenderhearted riders can save them from gratuitous thwacks if not from surreptitious pins.

At least 60 donkeys were stationed at various sheds on the hills, together with a few mules and ponies, kept for men to ride. The young donkey drivers tried to get a shilling for taking the well-to-do visitors up to the top of the hill, but were satisfied with rather less, charging half-price for the downward journey if their client did not want to walk down. Double price was charged for 'double-barrelled' donkeys equipped 'with panniers for those little trots who cannot be trusted to hold on to the pommels'. The writer of these passages visited Malvern on a particularly unusual day, 11 July 1861, when Charles Blondin, still basking in the glory of his astounding tightrope feats over the Niagara Falls in 1859, drew a sea of admirers to watch him perform at Pickersleigh. On that day the writer reckoned that each donkey – and its driver – covered 30 miles up and down the hills carrying the trippers; he concluded that it was fortunate that the Blondin day was an exception, 'the likes of which was never known since Malvern was a town'.

If you go down from the Worcestershire Beacon by the path which leads towards Great Malvern you will pass St Ann's Well, which has always been very popular, not least because it is relatively easy to reach from the town. A mushroom-like structure was added to the tiny well-house in the 19th century, which was enhanced in 1969 by wrought-iron gates. Designed by Catherine Moody, a local artist, and made by the local blacksmith, Dennis Morgan, they commemorate the much respected Joyce King, editor of the *Malvern Gazette* from 1945-65: her initials are at the centre of the design. Another much loved local character who is commemorated at the well is 'Blind George', George Pullen, who played his harmonium here every day for over 50 years, going into the well-house if it rained. His harmonium, which had a collecting box at one end, has been purchased by Malvern Museum, where it may be seen in a room upstairs.

The northern end of the hills was seriously damaged by quarrying, which continued here until 1970, but it has now been landscaped and planted by the Conservators. The community of North Malvern, like that at West Malvern, has a peculiarly village-like atmosphere of its own. Here and at the adjacent Link Top there was considerable encroachment of the common land in the 19th century when the Foley lords of the manor permitted a good number of modest houses to be built. Many of these later accommodated the quarrymen when the quarrying reached its peak in the early 20th century. Nowadays, modernised and often greatly extended, they offer many advantages not always found in modern buildings. From the mid-19th century onwards their inhabitants were provided with various facilities which today are considered essential but were then appreciated as luxuries. The Tank Quarry on North Hill, for example, took its name from the water-tanks paid for by Charles Morris so that as early as 1836 the people of North Malvern could have a decent water supply. To this day the tanks, crowned with a clock tower to mark Edward VII's accession in 1901, bear the following inscription: 'Ye young and aged poor pray that the blessings of God may be abundantly poured on him who has here poured abundant blessings upon you'.

Opposite the tanks a little school was built, also at the expense of Charles Morris, at a time when few people cared that most working people could neither read nor write. The school also received help from the National Society. It was subsequently extended and served the community very well up to 1991, the competence and devotion of its staff earning wide respect. In 1991 it was amalgamated with Cowleigh School, which had to be rebuilt following a serious fire. A little lower down the North Malvern Road, opposite the 19th-century Holy Trinity church, is a small enclosure with the old parish stocks and whipping post, once used to ridicule and punish offenders. Dishonest tradesmen are often seen as the prime victims of these ancient forms of punishment but there were also other unfortunates. For generations, before a national system of poor relief was available, help was obtained only from one's own parish and people who wandered in from other parishes ran the risk of being whipped before being sent back home if they dared to ask for help from a

50. The hills and commons provide opportunities for all kinds of enjoyment.

parish overseer other than their own. The whipping was usually administered at the parish boundary by the parish constable; like the overseers of the poor, constables were unpaid and elected to office at the annual parish meeting, the substantial householders taking it in turn to enjoy the doubtful honour – or shoulder its burden.

The southern end of the hills is much more picturesque and less densely populated than the northern. But it, too, was damaged by quarrying, the Gullet quarry being the last to close in 1977. Here, and in other places on the hills, as quarriers worked deeper into the ground they found it increasingly difficult to quarry profitably, one problem being that they reached the water-table and had to pump out water which seeped into the workings. As part of their centenary celebrations in 1984 the Conservators transformed the old Gullet quarry into a remarkable spot. As at Earnslaw, water was allowed to fill the cavity created by the quarrying, and peace and beauty came where once there had been noise, dirt and disfigurement. One novel feature was to leave exposed an area of geological interest, showing rock strata laid down in successive ages. The Malverns were formed in the pre-Cambrian period, perhaps as long as a thousand million years ago; later geological changes left several layers of different types of stone on top of the original granite, so they have much to tell the geologist.

This part of the hills may be reached from Castlemorton Common, sold to the Malvern Hills Conservators in the 1960s by its manorial lords, the Church Commissioners. The local inhabitants were not very happy about this, but now work in co-operation with the Conservators to preserve the very special character of this unspoilt region, with its wide variety of flora and fauna. They fervently hope that visitors will do the same. About two hundred acres here have been designated as a Site of Special Scientific Interest, of particular interest to bird lovers and botanists. It is a very popular area because it is easily accessible and offers excellent opportunities for family outings and picnics. Sometimes there is the added interest of watching hang-gliders taking off from the hills.

Further south still is Midsummer Hill with its iron-age fort. Of more modest dimensions than British Camp, it was excavated in the late 1960s by Dr. Stanford and his team from Birmingham University, who later published detailed records of their findings. Midsummer Hill is the only hill in the Malvern range not under the jurisdiction of the Conservators. It was given to the National Trust in 1923 by the Rev. and Mrs. H. Somers-Cocks, in memory of their son who had been killed in the First World War. The obelisk which may be seen a short distance away was erected much earlier by the Somers-Cocks family of Eastnor, in memory of other relatives who served their country in a variety of ways, some falling in earlier conflicts.

The next hill going south is Raggedstone Hill, with its legendary curse upon anyone on whom its shadow falls. The most southerly hill is Chase End Hill, with the Valley of the White Leaved Oak – meeting point of the three ancient counties of Gloucestershire, Herefordshire and Worcestershire – lying between it and Raggedstone Hill.

The hills and commons offer a wide variety of flora and fauna. Grassland is broken up by thickets of trees and clusters of blackberry, broom, gorse, bracken, heather and even bilberry. Sheep, ponies and goats are obviously put out to graze,

51. By providing good parking facilities at particular spots, the Malvern Hills Conservators concentrate visitor activity where it can be catered for and protect wildlife on the more vulnerable slopes.

but other animals find their natural habitat here, local gardeners sometimes grumbling at damage to their crops caused by the rabbits who shelter and breed so prolifically. Exploring the hills and commons around Malvern is the central point of a holiday for thousands of people; for others it is an opportunity to escape from the stresses of workaday life. For the most popular parts of the hills and commons there is rarely a respite from the constant pounding of feet – and yet, somehow, there are still idyllic spots which all can find, even if the Malvern natives remain tight-lipped about their own special places!

Chapter Eight

Elgar and Beauchamp Country

Elgar's biographer, Jerrold Northrop Moore, quotes a wonderfully evocative comment made by Elgar to a friend during his last illness. Whistling the main theme of his Cello Concerto, he said, 'If ever you are walking on the Malvern Hills and hear this, it's only me – don't be frightened'. This sums up the almost mystical relationship between Sir Edward Elgar and the county where he spent many of his best and most creative years. Some of his most moving music reflects his deep attachment to the scenes around him as he walked and bicycled through the countryside; and now, more than 50 years after his death, his native county, coming alive to the importance of this great composer, is paying him some of the tribute which was withheld in the earlier years.

52. The birthplace of Sir Edward Elgar. There are somewhat controversial plans to extend this museum to enable it to cope with increasing numbers of Elgar students and admirers.

53. Cattle are rarely seen grazing on the hills and commons now.

54. A winter view of the lodge at the entrance to Wynd's Point, former home of Jenny Lind.

There is so much connected with Elgar that may be seen in the area that in recent years an 'Elgar Trail' has evolved, complete with roadside signs to help the visitor. Booklets and even an audio tape may be purchased – the latter especially recommended for the real enthusiast who wants to spend time on an Elgar pilgrimage. This chapter aims at pointing out some of the more obvious places to visit, beginning with his birthplace, a small cottage in the village of Broadheath, two miles from Worcester. Elgar was born on 2 June 1857, the 17th birthday of Thomas Hardy, another great Englishman who commands enormous affection and grew to fame from modest rural roots. The fourth child of William and Ann Elgar, he spent only the first two years of his life at Broadheath; although his mother preferred the country, commitment to the family shop in Worcester necessitated a move back into the city. But the cottage at Broadheath exercised considerable influence over him and he enjoyed visiting it in later years, so it was particularly appropriate that, when

it came on to the market after his death, it should have been purchased to become a permanent memorial to him in the form of a delightful museum. Open daily, except Wednesdays, for most of the year, it contains a fascinating collection of photographs, manuscripts and all kinds of memorabilia, including his desk laid out with his spectacles and pens. A visit to this unique museum must be high on the list of priorities for anyone who has enjoyed Elgar's music, because the essence of the man is there in those tiny rooms.

The Elgar family kept a music shop in Worcester on a site now overrun by modern buildings. This was at the cathedral end of the High Street, facing the east end of St Helen's church, now part of the County Record Office. Elgar lived here with his family in rooms over the shop from 1863 until 1879. Close by is Worcester's impressive Guildhall, where in 1905 Elgar received the freedom of the city from the mayor, a lifelong friend from boyhood. Not far away, in 1981 Prince Charles unveiled a statue of the great musician looking towards the cathedral, which had so greatly influenced Elgar throughout his life.

55. Sir Edward Elgar looking towards the cathedral he knew so well, understandably turning his back on the desecration of the site of the family music shop which was his childhood home.

When he left school Elgar was to have become a lawyer, but about a year later, in 1873, he gave this up in order to help with the music shop, which advertised piano tuning among its services – a steady trade in the pre-television era when so many families liked to spend an evening round the piano. The young boy was immersed in music and soon began to stand in for his father as organist at St George's Catholic church, Sansome Place, Worcester, as well as playing a leading part in local musical groups. A couple of miles outside the city stood the formidable institution decreed necessary by an Act of Parliament in 1846 – the County Lunatic Asylum at Powick – which continued to be used for treatment of mental disorder until the 1980s. Treatment of the insane became more humane from the latter part of the 19th century and music was encouraged. From 1879 Elgar acted as musical director at the asylum, acquiring over the next five years valuable musical experience as both conductor and composer.

His modest income was augmented by giving music lessons. By the 1880s he made frequent visits to Malvern where he taught the violin at the numerous schools which were then springing up. Elgar enjoyed this no more than his young pupils, some of whom he reduced to tears. Some were, however, more rewarding than others: Miss Caroline Alice Roberts, daughter of an army officer, was regularly driven in her carriage from Hazeldine House in Redmarley to Malvern for lessons from Elgar, and she eventually became his wife. They were married in 1889, by which time both her parents were dead, but in that class-ridden age tongues wagged at the marriage between the impoverished son of a tradesman and a middle-class lady eight years his senior.

It was a good marriage, in which Alice was supportive and protective of the man in whose genius she never ceased to have faith, even ruling out manuscript pages in order to save money – an economy which must have come as a novel experience to one whose father had spent a lifetime being waited upon in India. The first year of their marriage was spent in London, hoping that Elgar's work would be more widely appreciated than in his own county. But the Elgars returned, disillusioned, to Worcestershire to live at Forli in Alexandra Road, Malvern Link until 1899, moving to Craeglea in the Wells Road, where they lived for the next five years. Craeglea is an anagram of the name Elgar with the initial letters of Edward, Alice and Carice. Carice was their only child, born in 1890, and her name was made up from the first and last syllables of her mother's two Christian names. Elgar was a founder of the Malvern Concert Club, which still exists, and during this period he composed prolifically, producing some of his most popular works, including the *Enigma Variations*, the *Dream of Gerontius*, *The Apostles* and the *Pomp and Circumstance Marches One and Two*. The latter, composed in 1901, has now become an emotional second national anthem with the words of 'Land of Hope and Glory', for occasions when our real one is deemed too sombre. It may be widely loved, but the words were not to Elgar's taste: amongst his varied emotions, jingoism was never apparent. From 1898 until 1903 the Elgars also took a summer home at Birchwood Lodge, four miles away in the rural peace of Storridge, looking towards the Malvern Hills from which he drew so much inspiration. All of these houses remain, but they are private homes and not open to the public.

By the turn of the century Elgar was becoming recognised at home and abroad, and began to be showered with academic and other honours, of which the chief

56. Gravestones: (a) Hydropathy did not seem to bestow longevity upon its pioneering Malvern practitioner: Dr. James Wilson died in his late 50s; (b) Twenty years later Jenny Lind was buried in Malvern cemetery; (c) A much simpler stone, designed by Troyte Griffith, marks the grave of Sir Edward Elgar and his wife in the churchyard of the 19th-century Roman Catholic church of St Wulstan in Malvern Wells.

57. An evocative view of a gas-lamp in Great Malvern priory churchyard.

were his knighthood conferred by Edward VII, and the Order of Merit by George V in 1911. It was an astonishing accomplishment for a self-taught musician from a small provincial city. In 1904 he moved with his family to Plas Gwyn, Vineyard Road, Hereford and then moved to Hampstead in 1912, where they lived until Lady Elgar's death in 1920. Having lost her devoted encouragement he, now in his mid-60s, began to rest on his laurels. He sold their London home, retaining a flat in St James' Place until 1929, and spent most of his last years in his native Worcestershire. He died at his home, Marl Bank, Rainbow Hill, Worcester on 23 February 1934, aged seventy-six. He was buried with his wife in the graveyard of St Wulstan's Roman Catholic church at Little Malvern, beneath the stone designed by his old friend, Troyte Griffith, the subject of the seventh Enigma variation.

The 13th variation was for many years believed to have been dedicated to Lady Mary Lygon, sister of the seventh Lord Beauchamp. Recent research by Cora Weaver and others suggests that in fact the subject of that Variation was the young woman to whom Elgar was engaged for over a year, Helen Weaver. However, he certainly had a friendship with Lady Mary Lygon and knew members of her family who lived at Madresfield Court. This beautiful, red-brick moated Tudor House has been the home of the Lygon family for 400 years and has never been open to the public, though its grounds and maze have traditionally been opened for a summer show every year. Evelyn Waugh visited the house and it became the model for his 'Brideshead'. When the eighth earl died in 1979 his widow continued to live in the house which both had loved so much; on her death in 1989, there being no children, uncertainty lay over the estate. In the summer of 1991 it was announced that, in accordance with the wishes of the earl and countess, a Beauchamp centre would be set up in order to foster the arts and preserve the house and its contents. The house would continue to be a home, inhabited by the niece of the eighth earl and her husband. The founder director of the arts centre would be the grandson of the countess through her first marriage, she having been widowed in her 20s.

Although at the time of going to press there is some doubt about the details of this scheme, its announcement aroused great interest and relief, for Madresfield is an historic estate, holding particular interest for the people of Malvern. During the Second World War numerous Malvern people were vetted, with a view to their working at Madresfield Court in the event of the war causing the royal family to move there from London. This never happened. Madresfield acquired something of an aura of mystery, the Beauchamps being a retiring couple who cared about the area in which they lived but did not seek publicity. Lady Beauchamp might be glimpsed doing her shopping or riding on her tricycle around her grounds, in which she took active interest until she died at the age of ninety-four. As her grandson commented when she died, she had 'the knack of combining all the dignity of a grand dame with a down-to-earth sense of humour and zest for life ... her favourite motto which is inscribed on one of the sundials at Madresfield Court was "That day is wasted on which we have not laughed"'.

At Newland, just off the A449 from Worcester to Malvern, lie the peaceful collegiate-style buildings which accommodate the Beauchamp Community. Their history is closely tied up with the Beauchamp family and the Victorian gothic design, by

58.   Madresfield Court, for centuries the home of the Beauchamp family.

P. C. Hardwick, arouses interest though, since they are the homes of numerous elderly people, they are not open to the public except by prior agreement with the administrator.

In 1847 the third Earl Beauchamp, carrying out the wishes of his wife Charlotte who had died some years earlier, left £60,000 for the building of almshouses at New-land, near to the Madresfield estate, so that former estate workers could enjoy an honourable retirement and not need recourse to the workhouse. Next to these brick almshouses a new stone church was built, also to the design of Hardwick. Unfortunately the unusual old timbered church in Newland, dedicated to St Leonard, was demolished, a cross now marking its site. The lychgate for the new

59. The interior of Newland church is extraordinarily difficult to photograph but this is a good view taken by Sandra Porter for the *Malvern Gazette*. At the centre of the picture is the historic Norman font brought to Newland from the old church of St Thomas in Great Malvern.

church was supposed to have been built from part of the materials of the original church, and the chancel of the old church was incorporated into the almshouse complex as a mortuary chapel. The new church acquired the historic 12th-century font. It had been brought to Newland 300 years earlier from the church of St Thomas, when the people of Great Malvern bought the priory church and abandoned St Thomas'. On its 19th-century marble base this simple Norman font contrasts well with the richly decorated church, which has maintained strong links with the Anglo-Catholic tradition of Keble and others who influenced the founders. The Beauchamp Community is in the hands of a board of trustees who deal with applications for apartments, which are now for the benefit of rent-paying communicant members of the Church of England – with special regard for those who have served others during their working lives.

The village of Madresfield itself owes much to the influence of the architect Frederick Preedy. Madresfield's original Norman church was taken down and replaced in 1852 by one designed by Pugin the younger shortly before his death. This church did not last long; having been built without proper foundations, it had to be demolished. Some might have seen this as divine, if posthumous, retribution for Pugin's uncharitable remarks about the early 19th-century work on Malvern priory church. The good people of Madresfield tried a new architect in 1866. Preedy, Worcestershire born, had established a reputation not only for designing churches but also for designing and making stained glass with which to embellish them. He loved to imitate the 14th-century gothic style and obtained commissions throughout the country. Worcestershire is rich in his work, his first major undertaking being the church of St John the Evangelist at Storridge, where he also designed the stained glass. This was built in 1856 just within the borders of the large parish of Cradley, with its genuinely medieval church. At Madresfield he designed the new church dedicated to St Mary and then, in 1868, the village school and several cottages. He favoured the gothic style in his schools as well as his churches – the schools at Powick and Callow End were his work, the latter paid for by Earl Beauchamp and doing double duty by serving as a church on Sundays.

Chapter Nine

Village Scenes

Many of the villages around the Malverns were once within the boundaries of Malvern Chase. Some, like Castlemorton, still retain some of the physical characteristics of the medieval forest, in which there were great tracts of open scrubland, and isolated homes nestling comfortably into scenery where time stood still. Other villages have changed almost beyond recognition, though none so much as Great Malvern itself.

The seat of administration of Malvern Chase was Hanley Castle, the centre of which has retained much of its charm. This parish was originally very extensive, stretching from the River Severn up to the top of Worcestershire Beacon. It did not get its present name until the 13th century, when King John, that maligned monarch who loved Worcestershire and chose its cathedral for his burial place, ordered a castle to be built in the middle of the forest which had given him so much pleasure during his life.

The parish was known as Potters' Hanley because in the Middle Ages it supported a flourishing pottery trade, its wares being transported to towns and villages along that great medieval thoroughfare, the River Severn. In 1573 John Hornyold, a leading local landowner, wrote 'nowe thei sell abrode to Glouc., Worcetor, Bristowe and other places as much bricke, tyle, erthen pottes ... as thei can possible make, wch is grete, because thei have the trees'. Fragments of broken pottery still turn up quite frequently in the gardens of the now quite densely populated village. One of the excitements of the 1980s has been an attempt to track down the sites of kilns, an activity which has so far met with only limited success. The potters were supposed to pay for licences to dig clay and fell trees to fire their kilns, though Hornyold implied that by the 16th century they evaded this. He also alleged that large numbers of trees had been felled, though only 15 years earlier, he claimed, 'the grete okes were so thick together that a wayne could not passe but in certaine places'. The area to which he referred appears to have been where the Three Counties Showground is now sited – a spot so remarkably devoid of trees as to suggest enormous activity in the past four centuries, as indeed there has been.

Hanley was the second of the 13 villages of Malvern Chase to enclose its common land. Fraught with legal niceties, its Enclosure Act was passed in 1797 and confirmed in power three great landowners, the Hornyolds, the Lechmeres and the Church. When the enclosure commissioners arrived with their surveying instruments they had, as part of their task, to make provision for new roads to serve the new fields. Cutting through the former common land, they could achieve every roadmaker's dream – uncomplicated straight lengths of road. If you are a visitor who does not know this area, it is worth bearing in mind that the B4208, an enclosure road, should be negotiated with caution, as its junction with the B4209 at the corner of the Three Counties Showground is, despite repeated attempts at improvement, one of the most notorious accident blackspots in the area.

The Three Counties Agricultural Society, which holds a show every June, was created by the amalgamation in 1922 of three older societies based on the county towns of Gloucester, Hereford and Worcester. Until the late 1950s the three counties took it in turns to organise the annual shows on various sites in their particular county. As the shows became more comprehensive in content, offering as much for the town-dweller as for the farmer, it became increasingly difficult to find suitable sites. The number of people attending, coupled with modern demands for better facilities, meant that serious thought had to be given to the acquisition of a permanent site. In view of the practical problems and the delicate issue of not upsetting the inhabitants of the county in which such a site might *not* be found, the problem of finding a permanent site looked impossible to solve. When some suitable land came up for sale in Worcestershire, only about a mile from the Herefordshire border, it must have seemed little short of miraculous, especially since the Malvern Hills provided a splendid backcloth to a ground with good access roads and ample

60. Gateposts at the entrance to Severn End, ancestral home of the Lechmere family, are topped with pelicans pecking their breasts. This is part of the crest of the family which has lived in Hanley since the Norman conquest.

parking. This new permanent site, first used in 1958, has enormous advantages, not least that it can be regularly improved. It is also a major asset for the Society which rents it out for events during the year, thus ensuring that it never lies idle. People come for all kinds of events from pony shows to Christian crusading ventures. This site, once described by John Hornyold as the 'verie harte' of Malvern Chase is now the very heart of the three counties, for, despite amalgamation of Herefordshire and Worcestershire in 1972, the partners in that arranged marriage still see themselves as two separate counties!

This part of the old parish of Hanley Castle is now known as Malvern Wells. The heart of the old parish lies three miles away in the picturesque cul-de-sac known as Church End, off the B4211, opposite the entrance to the privately owned Severn End. This entrance is recognisable by its pillars topped with the pelican from the crest of the Lechmere family, who for centuries lived at the timber-framed mansion. Church End epitomises south-west Worcestershire, once summed up by a planning officer as 'all red-brick and black-and-white'! A magnificent cedar tree stands in the centre of a picture framed in black and white houses, the scene completed by all the

61. Church End, Hanley Castle, from the tower of St Mary's church. In the centre the war memorial, with its medieval shaft, stands by the main entrance to the churchyard. The large black and white building, with its five gables, is now in private ownership but was once the village almshouses.

62.   The reservoir at British Camp.

63.   The ancient hill-fort of British Camp.

necessary features of village life – a beautiful church, the village pub and one of the oldest schools in the country (though the 1326 claimed on its front by enthusiastic restorers in the 1930s is probably 100 years too optimistic).

The oldest part of the school is the black and white wing to the right, facing the church: the now blocked-up doorway, visible from the churchyard, carries a barely decipherable inscription of 1733 acknowledging its restoration by the schoolmaster, James Brooke, and the Lechmere landowners, whose pelican symbol has been the badge of the school for generations. The school has gone through many vicissitudes in its long history, enjoying a usually favourable reputation, though there were some controversial moments, especially in the 18th century, when the teacher was apt to fall asleep in class and one pupil 'could scarce write his own name' after five years in the school. By the turn of the present century it was a grammar school for boys, several of whom were boarders. Since a reorganisation of education in the area in 1974 it has been a co-educational high school, serving many of the surrounding villages.

The church of St Mary is an idyll of warm brick set in a well-kept churchyard, whose first point of interest is the war memorial containing the shaft of a medieval cross. The church itself is basically a late Norman building, much altered over the years. There is a nave and an aisle, each with its own gabled roof, and a rather squat

64. St Mary's church, Hanley Castle, from the south.

square tower built in the 17th century, though looking somewhat Norman. The castle was about a quarter of a mile to the south of this church and can be reached via a footpath. But there is nothing left, apart from its name, except the remains of the moat and a small mound of earth; the castle's remaining tower was used in 1795 to repair a bridge over Poolbrook, which runs into the River Severn.

On leaving Church End you can turn right and travel the few hundred yards into Upton, dealt with in a separate chapter, or left towards the Rhydd and Guarlford, an attractive if straggling parish formed in the 19th century from an outlying part of Malvern. The Rhydd is an historic junction where medieval forest offenders were sometimes hanged – a dubious distinction reserved for the inhabitants of Hanley, lesser mortals being despatched elsewhere. You may choose to turn off before reaching the Rhydd, on to the B4209, known locally as Robert's End Street, an old turnpike road leading back to the Three Counties Showground and up to the hills. Almost immediately, on the left, is the winding road to Gilbert's End, probably named after a 13th-century forester who lived there. 'End' was simply a settlement within the forest and Hanley has several of them, for example Hayler's End, Picken End and Church End. The spot where Robert's End Street, Gilbert's End Lane and the main B4211 Upton to Worcester road meet was possibly the site of the medieval markets held in Hanley. Old records refer to it as the Booth Hall, Buthall or Boothend so it may well have been the site of the toll booth, where merchants paid their market dues and swindlers were brought to a speedy trial in the Pie Powder court. The curious little structure at the opening into Gilbert's End Lane simply protects the pump which was so vital in village life before the advent of piped water into homes. Robert's End was probably the area where the medieval potters were active, though this is a subject which is likely to occupy researchers for many years yet. Hanley Swan boasts an attractive pool and a pub overlooking the village green, where the oak planted in 1863 to mark the marriage of the future Edward VII to Princess Alexandra of Denmark has now reached magnificent maturity. The pub is older than the name Hanley Swan; the area was once called Swan Green and local oral tradition claims that Hanley Swan was adopted only when the telephone exchange was set up and needed a name!

At the centre of Hanley Swan some visitors will take the turning for the caravan park at Blackmore Park, the nucleus of the empire once owned by the powerful Hornyold family. They were, like the Russells and the Beringtons of Little Malvern, a Catholic family who fostered their religion in private until the Roman Catholic Emancipation Act in 1829 enabled them to support it publicly. The great church dedicated to St Mary and St Alphonsus, close to their home in Blackmore Park, was one result. Blackmore House itself was demolished, the present house, which is private, being a 20th-century structure. However, parts of the old house still exist: for example, Malvern Girls' College bought the imposing porch and re-erected it as the entrance to the 1934 extension built at the back of Elmslie's *Imperial Hotel*.

From Hanley Swan you turn towards Welland and Castlemorton for the attractive country route to Gloucester. Welland Animal and Bird Gardens are open daily and include a pets' corner for children. Welland was enclosed in 1852, thus emphasising the shifting of most of its population away from the original small church, which

65. Eastnor Castle from the south, showing the terrace.

66. Modern craftsmanship – a porcelain owl by Boehm of Malvern.

67. The *Swan* at Hanley Swan, viewed from across the pond. This area used to be known as Swan Green; the green itself is dominated by a spectacular oak tree, while the old village pound used to stand to the left of the pond.

had been built in the medieval period on the boundary with Upton parish. A Victorian church was opened in 1875 opposite the *Pheasant Inn* so providing the social and spiritual needs of a village now focused closer to the hills, some of which, overlooking the parish, were marked on a 17th-century map as the Welland Hills.

A few hundred yards beyond Welland church is Castlemorton, already mentioned in the chapter on the hills and commons. It is a reminder of the medieval terrain and offers all the pleasures of open countryside to families and walkers, though the local farmers are understandably keen to make them aware that the animals grazing on the common are their livelihood and should be treated with respect. Visitors do not always realise that the sheep have an historic right to wander on the road.

We now go on to Birtsmorton, with its moated court house (no longer open to the public) and its Waterfowl Sanctuary which is worth a visit. From here it is possible to take country roads to numerous pleasant spots. One such drive might take us out of Worcestershire to the peaceful and historic parish of Deerhurst in north Gloucestershire. Its early history is not entirely clear, but its monastery may have been attacked by the Danes. There is also the myth that it was from here that St Werstan came to Malvern and founded a new priory. Whatever happened in those distant years, it is certain that Deerhurst is now doubly lucky in possessing not one but two Saxon churches. In this forest of wild animals – the literal meaning of

68.   Feeding the ducks at Castlemorton.

Deerhurst – Edward the Confessor's supporter, Earl Odda, dedicated a royal hall and chapel in 1056, opposite the gateway to the priory church used by monks possibly as long ago as the seventh century. The monks' church, naturally modified over the centuries, became the parish church at the time of the dissolution of the monasteries and has remained so since. It is impossible to describe the aura of Deerhurst. Its peace, historical associations and relics such as the magnificent Saxon font and unique Saxon windows are strangely moving.

A few miles west of Deerhurst lies Staunton, reputedly the home of Dick Whittington. Since this story lacks documentation it is perhaps safer to leap forward a few hundred years to its 19th-century Chartist associations, for which there is much evidence. The Chartists agitated for parliamentary reform, their Charter demanding six points: universal manhood suffrage, equal constituencies, secret ballot, payment of M.P.s, abolition of the property qualification for M.P.s and annual elections. These Chartist ideas were much in advance of their times, but ultimately all except the last of their demands were realised. Like the Suffragettes, who came about seventy years later, the Chartists alerted those in authority to the seething resentment felt by great sections of the population but they failed actually to deliver what their rank and file members wanted. That satisfaction being denied to them, the credit for reform, when it eventually came, went to politicians who had the sense to recognise where their own best interests lay.

One of the Chartist leaders, Feargus O'Connor, pursued a scheme to move families struggling in the factory towns to rural smallholdings where they could be self-sufficient. Two estates comprising between them about 130 of these smallholdings were set up in the late 1840s in this part of the Midlands: Lowbands is actually in Worcestershire, but the other one was around Staunton in Gloucestershire, at Snigs End and Moat Lane. These settlements were doomed to failure. Many people put money into the Chartist Land Company to buy land, but in the lottery to allocate smallholdings only a few hundred lucky ones were awarded land and their entitlement to it was not supported in law. The Company was investigated and wound up within 10 years, many of the occupiers of land losing the means of livelihood to which they had gone with such high hopes. The 19th-century chronicler of Worcestershire, T. C. Turberville, wrote a damning indictment of the whole affair at the time that the company was under investigation:

> The National Land Scheme, under which this estate, with others in different parts of the country, was purchased, set out into lots, and divided to the few drawers of prizes in a lottery to which thousands of others had subscribed, was one of the hugest delusions to which the working men of this country ever lent themselves under demagogue leadership. They allowed themselves to be persuaded, not only that to leave their manual handicraft and become squatters on an acre or two of ground would be the climax of independence and happiness, but that by some legerdemain of compound interest, their money and estates would be so reproductive that all the subscribers would in a few years get allotments, which, being freehold, would give them immense political power. The fortunate allottees soon found that they did not hold the fee simple of their acres, but were called upon by O'Connor to pay a large rent, and being unaccustomed to husbandry, were speedily reduced to the condition of ruined paupers, subsistent on the charity of the farmers among whom they were located.

O'Connor himself was declared insane in 1852 and the company collapsed with the results that Turberville indicated, but many of the well-built and now modernised houses have survived and are still inhabited. It is intriguing to see them set at an angle along the road to Gloucester, all obviously built to more or less the same plan and set in spacious plots.

Chapter Ten

Upton: A Severnside Town

Some seven miles from Malvern lies Upton-upon-Severn, a small town which once greatly overshadowed Malvern. Upton is well worth exploring on foot: the basic plan of its alleys and streets has scarcely changed since medieval times when it was a flourishing market town serving 20 or more surrounding villages. People walked or rode in from miles around to buy or sell their eggs, butter, cheese, cattle, sheep – and even themselves. For at Upton there were regular 'mop' fairs at which labourers might be hired. The streets were filled with people, animals, noise and dirt. Although the old markets have long since disappeared, behind the High Street, on a modern housing development, some tethering rings have been preserved in a wall as a token reminder of a world we have lost.

If you approach the town, as most people do, along the B4211 from Worcester you will know you are getting close when you see the green copper-covered cupola of its medieval tower in front of you. This, nicknamed the Pepperpot, is Upton's landmark; last surviving remnant of the medieval church, the tower is a good place from which to begin a walk around the town.

The old church was damaged, like so many in this part of Worcestershire, during the civil war in the 17th century. Soldiers fought in the narrow streets of Upton and in its churchyard, damaging both the church and the stone bridge over the river. This has now disappeared, but bridge abutments may be seen a little further down the river from the present hideous bridge; one can imagine the picturesque sandstone structure which, in varying states of repair, served from 1605 until 1852. Do not be carried away with the romance of it all – there is evidence that it was unkempt and even from time to time used by an enterprising Uptonian as a pig-sty, presumably keeping his animals in the convenient passing bays.

Oliver Cromwell believed that if his forces had not won the Battle of Upton in the summer of 1651 then he would have been unable to secure the 'crowning mercy' of defeating the future Charles II at Worcester a few days later. He came to Upton to thank the townsfolk; some people believe that he spoke to them in the cottages now known as Cromwells, facing the Pepperpot, though there is no documentary evidence to support this, the name not having appeared until the 1970s.

This part of Upton is at the very heart of the town's history and sited at the edge of the feature which made Upton so prosperous in the past – the River Severn. The Severn was for centuries one of the most important waterways in Europe, carrying such vital commodities as salt from Droitwich, corn, coal, cider and the bishop of Hereford's supply of French wine from Bristol! Many Upton men earned their living from the river, some rather dubiously, by stretching nets across it to catch salmon 'of unsizeable lengths and at unseasonable times' to sell at a vast profit. But many a hard and honest living was made in boat-building, loading and unloading cargoes and hauling trows – the barges which were the most common means of transport up

69. Tethering rings remind us of Upton's past as a
market town.

and down the river. The last surviving trow, the *Spry*, has been rescued from its
watery grave in Worcester's Diglis Basin and restored at the Ironbridge Gorge
Museum; plans are now in hand to take it to the maritime museum in Bristol. Hauling trows was very thirsty work, which perhaps helps to explain the large number of
inns and public houses in towns and villages along the riverbank.

Although the river brought jobs and commercial advantage, there were problems
too. The design of early bridges impeded the flow of water, and freezing over was

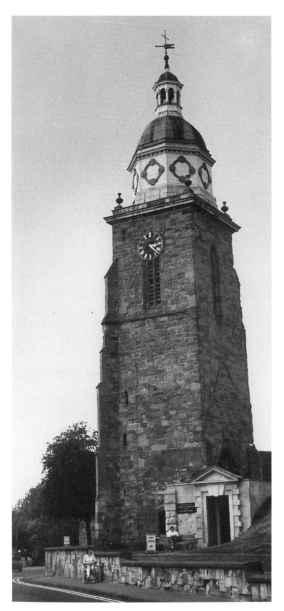

70. The medieval church tower at Upton-on-Severn is popularly known as the Pepperpot. At the base are the tourist information office and heritage centre.

quite common in the winter months. When the thaw set in, flooding followed and still occurs from time to time, though modern weather forecasting and drainage have minimised the distress caused. Modern inhabitants, too, are no longer huddled together in the overcrowded and low-lying alleyways, which in 1832 were the scene of a devastating outbreak of cholera – the consequence of medical ignorance coupled with unhygienic living conditions.

In the 18th century the main body of the church, never properly repaired after the Battle of Upton, was taken down and replaced, but the medieval tower was retained. Some years later a cupola was put on the tower, from which the original spire had been removed. By the 19th century its resemblance to 'a colossal pepper box' provided the nickname it bears today. Despite repeated problems with the cupola, it survived the test of time better than the 18th-century body of the church, which was far too small for the Victorian population of Upton. In 1879 the present church at the far end of Old Street was consecrated. The old riverside church was allowed to decay and was eventually demolished in the late 1930s, but the tower still remained – a haven for pigeons and a landmark for miles around. In the 1980s it was thoroughly overhauled to serve the needs of 20th-century tourism; a tourist information centre was established on part of the site of the old church nave, and the base of the tower was adapted for an exhibition of Upton's history.

When you wander through the streets in the centre of Upton, it is a good idea to look up to the first and second floors to see how the buildings looked before modern retailers gave their ground floor a facelift. Some of the oldest properties are in traditional black and white, but considerable change took place in the 18th and 19th centuries, when classical and Georgian façades were built on to earlier timber-

71. The River Severn, which played so large a part in establishing Upton's historic importance, reflects its main landmark, the Pepperpot. Its hideous modern bridge, towards the right, replaced a bridge which spanned the river from the bottom of the High Street (from the steps of the far bank) to the point on the near bank from which the picture was taken.

framed structures by fashion conscious businessmen trying to impress with their good taste and financial success. But they often covered up craftsmanship which dates from medieval times, when New Street really was a new development of shops and houses distinct from that in the original main street – Old Street. In Old Street we can still detect the hallmark of a medieval town with long, narrow burgage plots, enabling as many tradesmen as possible to enjoy the commercial advantage of a frontage on the main road. As time went on, many of these plots were sub-divided, with quite different businesses being carried on in the rear, alleyways between the plots giving access to them. This arrangement can also be seen in other local towns, such as Tewkesbury and Ledbury.

Upton had another feature similar to Ledbury: in the wedge-shaped High Street, near the present *White Lion Hotel*, stood a black and white market house on stilts. It was an early victim of road improvement, disappearing in the 18th century when the new turnpike roads into the town brought increased traffic: the dilapidated old building, with its dangerous steps, was in the way as coaches changed horses, dropped or picked up passengers at the inns, or simply thundered down Old Street, through the High Street and straight on over the old bridge. (The siting of the modern bridge is one of the few major changes in the layout of roads in the centre of Upton.) A proliferation of turnpike acts in the 18th century with the resultant boom in road building meant that coaching inns did a good trade. In Upton *The Star* and *The White Lion* were coaching inns, the latter featuring as the inn in which Fielding set his novel *Tom Jones*. A less happy distinction attended *The Anchor* in 1831, when body-snatching was rife due to the shortage of bodies for training doctors; two newly buried bodies were despatched in packing cases from this inn to London. Fortunately discovered in time, they were restored to their resting places in Hanley Castle churchyard, but the culprits were not detected.

There are some other reminders of a past which was not so pleasant as the romantic would have us believe. If you walk to the end of New Street you will see a plaque marking the site of two cottages known as the Goom Stool Cottages. Presumably they had a particularly good view of that degrading punishment, the ducking-stool, known locally as the gum or goom stool. There was a small lake which probably served as the town's rubbish dump, into which nagging wives and dishonest tradesmen were reputedly dipped, though records of Upton's manorial courts indicate that the town often lacked a ducking-stool. After winter floods, water still lies on the sports field, just behind the old fire station at the end of New Street: perhaps this was the dreaded goom-stool lake.

Continuing your walk, about half a mile out of town beyond the end of New Street, a footpath to the left takes you off the winding country road to the desolate

72. Traditional black and white architecture in the heart of Upton. To the left is the old market cross, now part of the town's war memorial.

spot where terrified survivors of Upton's cholera epidemic unceremoniously buried their dead in that grim summer of 1832. A low brick wall, with commemorative plaque, marks the rectangular burial ground which was used for all but the first few burials, after fears were expressed about the wisdom of burying infected bodies in the churchyard in the middle of the town. This was of special significance in view of the standards of hygiene at the time; no form of official refuse collection existed until well into the 20th century, so people left piles of rubbish outside their homes. Animals of all kinds roamed around, rats and pigs being perhaps the most numerous. Pigs were a recognised feature of town life – there were complaints in the 18th century that they even rooted among the graves because the churchyard was inadequately protected from their inquisitive snouts.

Brickmaking used to be one of the industries of Upton, with extensive brickfields on the far side of the river. In the 1970s this area was transformed by the building of the marina which attracts hundreds of boating enthusiasts to Upton: the Severn thus continues to have an impact on the economy of the town, for the marina heralded the start of Upton's attempts to cater for tourists. The recognition of the need for tourist provision led in the 1980s to some unusual events becoming regular highlights in the town's summer calendar.

In 1985 Upton revived the interesting old custom of celebrating Oak Apple Day on 29 May, the birthday of Charles II. Oak trees have traditionally been associated with Charles II and his restoration to the monarchy in 1660 because of the story that he hid in an oak tree after the Battle of Worcester when he was fleeing from the Parliamentarians to safety on the continent. For about two hundred years churches, with varying degrees of enthusiasm, rang their bells or otherwise celebrated the restoration of the monarchy until the custom died out in the 19th century. But Upton never totally forgot it and there was particular interest shown some years ago in a drawing from an 1857 edition of the *Illustrated London News* which showed the people of Upton dancing in Dunn's Lane. The Dunn's Lane dance has been revived and Oak Apple Day has once more become an annual opportunity for jollification in Upton, with the added bonus of raising substantial sums for local charities. So if you are in Upton at the end of May don't be too surprised if you spot a town crier, smell a pig roast or get caught up in a rather special dance!

In June Upton holds its annual carnival, followed during the last weekend in June, by the annual jazz festival, which draws thousands of people from all over the country: shops, bars and businesses throughout the town enter into the spirit of this happy, relaxed occasion. A month later Upton's steam rally is a must for enthusiasts from far and wide. As well as vehicles, steam engines can be seen driving all kinds of machinery – threshing, grinding, sawing and stone-crushing. Fairground organs add to the nostalgia and festive atmosphere.

Not far from Upton, just across the Severn, is the pretty village of Ripple, with which Upton was surveyed in the Domesday Book. Its church dates from the 12th century: some of its walls have a disconcerting tendency to lean, but it is a delight, inside and out. There are similarities between this church and Great Malvern priory church, though it is much smaller. It has 16 superb misericords similar to those at the priory church and in the churchyard stands the remains of a cross. Malvern has

73. Oak Apple Day in Upton, 1991.

a complete, if rather peculiar hybrid cross in its churchyard, the late medieval base being surmounted by a 19th-century copy of an early medieval cross. Such crosses are sometimes called palm crosses because they incorporated a little niche to hold the consecrated bread and wine during the Palm Sunday procession. In 1229 the Bishop of Worcester required every parish in his diocese to erect such a 'fair and proper cross'. Ripple has retained some fragments of medieval glass from its east window but most was lost by the mid-17th century, probably as a result of a fire being lit on the altar by puritans trying to destroy the censer and other pieces associated with rituals of which they disapproved. Perhaps they were also responsible for the medieval font being used as a water-trough in a cowshed – it was rescued by the rector in the 1840s and restored. The west window was designed by Kempe, whose work may be found in other local churches, and the east by one of his pupils in the 1880s.

Around Upton lie several attractive villages and some quiet riverside spots approached by narrow country lanes – each explorer must find his own secret hideaway!

Chapter Eleven

Into Herefordshire

Some eight miles from Malvern, the little old market town of Ledbury is well worth a visit, as film-makers, hungry for shots of its Church Lane in a medieval time warp, have often decided. In the wedge-shaped centre of this 'little town of ancient grace' (John Masefield) is its market house built on oak (or possibly Spanish chestnut) pillars in the 17th century. The upper rooms were used as a corn market while the butter and poultry market was held in the covered area underneath. Nowadays a few stalls selling eggs, cheese, vegetables and other goods continue the market day tradition. Despite the widespread popularity of large supermarkets, Ledbury has a faithful army of shoppers who prefer the individuality and service offered by a wide variety of retail outlets clustered around the market-place and the roads leading to it. These roads include the Homend, the road at the ham, or meadow, end of the town, while the Southend is self-explanatory. New Street has been so named for hundreds of years, to distinguish it from the original High Street, and Bye Street is a corruption of the original Bishop Street, for Ledbury was part of the vast estate of the Bishop of Hereford, who had founded a market there in medieval times. Soon after the diocese of Hereford was formed at the end of the seventh century, several minster, or mother, churches were established as centres from which priests set out to spread the Christian gospel to the surrounding area. One of these was built in Ledbury, though the original modest structure was replaced soon after the Norman Conquest by a larger and more impressive building which was to be the nucleus of the present parish church.

This church, dedicated to St Michael and All Angels, is built mainly of sandstone and is large enough to hold over 1,000 people. The impression of size is reinforced by the fact that the north and south walls slope outwards, being supported by massive external buttresses. The oak roof timbers are medieval, though considerable modern restoration work has been necessary. In the chancel, above the typically rounded Norman arches, are unusual windows resembling port-holes, which originally ran the length of the church to form a clerestory overlooking the roof of the 12th-century side aisles. To the north, the lady chapel contains a memorial to Mr. and Mrs. Moulton Barrett, parents of Elizabeth Barrett Browning who spent much of her childhood at the family home, Hope End, just outside Ledbury. Although Hope End House was demolished at the end of the 19th century the coach house and stable block have been refurbished as a delightful country hotel serving home-grown produce. Elizabeth Barrett Browning herself is commemorated in the building which bears her name and accommodates the town library, opposite the market hall.

The stained glass is mostly 19th-century, but a large new window was designed and dedicated in 1991. The baptistry chapel is dedicated to St Katherine. There is

74. Church Lane, Ledbury, entices the tourist to explore the old buildings that line its gentle slope.

75. Ledbury's market house still causes controversy – are its pillars English oak or Spanish chestnut?

more than one St Katherine in the calendar of saints and local folklore has confused the matter further, so it is worth examining some of the stories about the origin of the dedication to St Katherine.

Legend says that the saintly and aristocratic Katherine Audley lived during the late 13th and early 14th centuries. Her family owned the house known as Hellens, at Much Marcle, some four miles outside Ledbury. Many legends are woven round Hellens, which is open to the public on some summer afternoons. While Lady Katherine was riding round to do good works accompanied by her maid, Mabel, her mare and colt were stolen. She found them at Ledbury by following the tracks left in the ground, and a hospital dedicated to St Katherine was founded on the spot where the animals were sheltering. A variation on the story is that Katherine Audley had vowed that she would not rest until she came to a town where the bells would ring by themselves; when she and Mabel came near Ledbury she heard the bells ringing, though no ringers were there. She spent her final years as a recluse some distance outside the town, continuing to lead a righteous and sober life, and surviving on a diet of herbs and milk from a farm called The Hazel. King Edward II granted her an annuity of £30 out of respect for her piety and noble birth. She has appeared in the literary work of both Wordsworth and John Masefield, who spent his formative early years in Ledbury and whose name was adopted for the comprehensive school established by the educational changes in the mid-1970s.

So what are we to make of the stories about Ledbury's St Katherine? Katherine Audley's story has romantic appeal but she was not the saint to whom the chapel was dedicated, as she was never canonised. The chapel may well have been built soon after her death, however, and its dedication to the saint whose name she shared would have had a particular significance. Close to the John Masefield High School is Mabel's Furlong. Possibly Mabel, Katherine's maid, rode regularly here, but so obvious an interpretation should probably be avoided, as place-name derivation is full of traps for the unwary. In the centre of the town is St Katherine's hospital, founded by Bishop Hugh Foliot in 1232, long before Katherine Audley was born.

St Katherine's hospital may have been built on the site of the original bishop's palace in Ledbury. Its purpose was the provision of both spiritual and earthly comfort for all in need – the sick, the poor, the old, the distressed and, of course, pilgrims and other travellers passing through the town. In our modern welfare state it is easy to forget the important role formerly played by the Church in caring for those who needed assistance. In the great hall of St Katherine's hospital those in need were cared for by a group of brethren under the control of a master. Such voluntary help was given in this way for centuries, though precise details of the system varied from time to time: in the 15th century the master, whose position caused him to enjoy some superior social standing, decided to occupy a separate part of the property, which has naturally been altered in various ways over the years. In 1822 new almshouses, facing the market house, were built to the plans of Sir Robert Smirke, who had recently been employed as the architect for Eastnor Castle, a couple of miles away. Restored in recent years, the ancient St Katherine's hospital foundation continues to serve Ledbury as a community centre.

Inns and pubs also serve important social purposes and Ledbury is well endowed with these establishments. One of the oldest is the *Feathers Hotel*, dating from Elizabethan times, and particularly important as a coaching inn. The passing of the Ledbury Turnpike Act in 1721 caused a great deal of ill feeling in the area. People who were scraping a living from the land bitterly resented the imposition of tolls on local roads, and riots occurred during the 1730s, the ringleaders being executed. But the road improvements brought prosperity to those operating coach services and to the inns supplying the needs of passengers, drivers and horses. In New Street the 16th-century *Old Talbot Inn* also served as a coaching inn. It contains fine old panelling, damaged by bullet holes when its warm welcome was insufficient to reconcile the differences between roundheads and cavaliers who met in one of its rooms after the Battle of Ledbury in 1645. This was one of the minor skirmishes of the Civil War, when Prince Rupert's men routed those of Colonel Massey but, even so, over 100 men were killed and several hundred injured. The names of some of Ledbury's oldest inns, the *Prince of Wales*, the *Feathers* and the *Royal Oak*, certainly have a royalist flavour and the town saw blood spilt on several occasions during the great struggle between king and parliament.

The original main crossroads in Ledbury was where Bye Street met the Homend and the High Street, the route continuing up towards the church. In the 18th century Top Cross, the present main crossroads with traffic lights, assumed more importance and the old rural-sounding name Horse Lane became the unimaginative

Worcester Road, though the small modern housing estate built in the 1960s preserved the link with the past, for it was called Horse Lane Orchard. During the middle ages the bishops of Hereford had a palace and acres of parkland here at the top end of town, but economic problems of the later medieval period caused the palace to be neglected and it fell into ruin. In the late 16th century a grand new house, known as Ledbury Park, was built and was reputedly used by Prince Rupert as his headquarters during the Civil War. Opposite Ledbury Park is the 'house on props', these props being similar to the pillars supporting the market house. In view of the number of heavy lorries which have rumbled through the streets of Ledbury, it is quite remarkable that this vulnerable build-ing, with its upper storey projecting out into the narrowest part of New Street, has survived.

76. The *Feathers Hotel* in Ledbury.

One of the most picturesque parts of Ledbury is Church Lane, its cobbled path leading from the market house up to the church. On the right is a timber-framed building which has suffered the indignity of two removals. Many people can remember it standing at the rear of Boot's the chemist in the High Street, but its original home was in the middle of the High Street, when it formed part of the Butcher's Row, most of which was demolished in the early 19th century. This demolition served two purposes: to ease traffic congestion and to clean up the unsavoury town centre, where public slaugh-tering of animals still seemed to be taking place. The Butcher Row House Museum is well worth a visit, as is the Old Grammar School Heritage Centre on the opposite side of Church Lane.

The Old Grammar School was opened to the public after restoration in 1978. It dates from the late medieval period, when it was probably used as a guildhall for wool merchants, becoming a grammar school some time later, perhaps in the 17th century. Such schools were often founded by tradesmen keen to educate their sons, though little is known about the establishment of this one, which seems to have gone by the middle of the 19th century, when the building was empty and in poor condition.

At the top of Church Lane is Rutherglen, a superb 18th-century brick house which, in the 19th century, was reduced to serving as the police station, with magistrates' court and cells for the accused. At least this was preferable to the neglect it suffered in the present century. Opposite are the lovely old Abbot's Lodge and Church House.

Beyond the church are Upper Hall and Nether Hall, estates originally intended for the benefit of the two portionists, the clergymen who once shared the income from the church in Ledbury. These delightful grounds and buildings are unfortunately not open to the public, but since Upper Hall served as one of Herefordshire's co-educational grammar schools from 1921, many of the inhabitants of Ledbury are very well acquainted with the house and grounds. Many of its original features, such as ceiling mouldings and fireplaces, were retained and all who worked there, staff and pupils alike, felt lucky to be in one of the most beautifully situated schools in the country. In the mid-1970s it became the junior part of the comprehensive school provision for the Ledbury area, but falling rolls led to its closure in the summer of 1991. A question mark now (1992) lies over this property; many people hope that it will provide some kind of community centre for the town, so maybe by the time you read this book you *will* be able to see inside.

Between Ledbury and Malvern lies the village of Eastnor, with its castle dating from 1812 and built to resemble a medieval stronghold. Sir Robert Smirke designed it for the first Earl Somers, whose descendants still live in it. Indeed, if you book a party visit at the right time you may be able to enjoy a meal with them in the elegant dining room of the castle! Alternatively you are welcome to picnic in the grounds. Beyond the castle lake is a 300-acre deer park, where red deer occupy land which has been designated a Site of Special Scientific Interest because of the wildlife which flourishes there. The castle and its grounds have been used in numerous films and television programmes, including *The Pallisers*. The first earl also had a great obelisk erected in the park, visible for miles around, to commemorate various members of his family: John, Lord Somers, held high office in the reigns of William III and Queen Anne; James Cocks died in 1758, fighting in the Seven Years' War; and in 1812 Major Edward Charles Cocks, the eldest son of the man who caused the memorial to be made, died as he rallied his troops during the Peninsular War.

Another interesting old town within the area administered by Malvern Hills District Council is Bromyard, unfortunately too often overlooked by the visitor. Like Upton-upon-Severn some years ago, the town used to have a somewhat forgotten, almost neglected image but is now more aware of its real potential and is seeking to emulate the success of Upton in regenerating itself by responding to modern demands.

Like Ledbury, Bromyard was an important missionary centre with a minster church from which Christianity spread into the surrounding countryside. Of its original Saxon church nothing now remains, but the present church dedicated to St Peter dates from Norman times, though it has been considerably enlarged and embellished over the centuries. Its south doorway is an especial delight, with its rounded Norman arch showing three quite distinct decorative forms, while the door itself is of the later, Gothic style. Above this interesting array of architectural styles is a carved figure, believed to be a Saxon representation of St Peter with the keys of heaven.

77. Upper Hall, Ledbury, was a school for 70 years until 1991. The oldest part, on the left, dates from the 17th century and the central sections are 18th century. In the 19th century the right-hand side of the building, with spacious bays, was added.

Some of the secular buildings in Bromyard also originated in the medieval period when bustling activity filled its streets. The manor of Bromyard belonged to the bishopric of Hereford so, like Ledbury, it benefited from the business acumen of bishops who laid out new streets and nursed the little settlement into a flourishing town. The close relationship between religious and secular life, which was permeated by the Church's teaching, is also symbolised by the fact that it is in the church, at the back, that a bushel measure is still kept after being used for many years as a water-butt and then as a fireside log container. A bushel reminds some of us of the complicated tables of weights and measures which plagued our young schooldays before the simpler metric tables were introduced. For fair trading it was obviously essential to standardise volume measures as well as weights, so Bromyard's measure, dating from 1670, was once readily available for use on market day.

The hub of the medieval town was the market square where stalls were erected on market day. Bromyard's market square was dominated by the old market hall which stood until the 19th century in front of the *Hop Pole Hotel*, built in the Georgian period. This period, the late 18th and early 19th centuries, saw considerable modernisation of the frontages of ancient property as successful householders proclaimed their prosperity to friends and neighbours. The town's early history is concealed behind these frontages and in the cellars and attics of shops and houses, unfortunately not accessible to the visitor.

Small market towns such as Bromyard, Ledbury and Upton were important in establishing Britain's economic stability. Such towns were focal points, serving the needs of surrounding rural parishes. Bromyard hiring fair, the mop, took place every 1 May. On these occasions farmers would look for labourers, while men and women seeking employment would wear or carry some item related to their trade. A shepherd might carry a crook, as did Gabriel Oak in Hardy's *Far from the Madding Crowd.*

Market towns served the surrounding area but were also dependent on it for food and other supplies. Bromyard's new Heritage Centre is largely devoted to the history of one such local commodity – hops. Hop farms were a particular characteristic of this region, providing the livelihoods of countless numbers of local farmers and their labourers. For generations they also provided a welcome break for hard-pressed workers in the new industrial towns; they were only too happy to meet the demand of local farmers for seasonal workers to pick hops. In an age which knew nothing of paid holidays, such workers could not afford the luxury of taking time off to relax but they could, and did, come to the countryside to enjoy the fresh air and at the same time earn some money.

78. The splendid entrance to Bromyard church, with its rich variety of designs embellishing the typically Norman arch.

Towns were open to new ideas brought in by travellers and merchants, so Protestant Nonconformists were naturally more numerous in towns than in the country areas. While Upton-upon-Severn had its Baptists in the 17th century, Bromyard had its Congregationalists a few years later, their minister housed in a manse behind his church. The medieval monopoly of Roman Catholicism was successfully challenged at the end of the Middle Ages, but to some people the religious changes introduced by the Tudor monarchs were not radical enough. Since the church settlement, the *via media*, of Elizabeth I aimed at embracing as many of her subjects as possible and put the monarch at the head of the Church of England, those who did not conform were regarded as a potential threat to the stability of the government and required special permission to build their churches. Roman Catholics were viewed with especial suspicion; the Gunpowder Plot by Catholics in 1605 and the attempt to put the Catholic Bonnie Prince Charlie on the throne in 1745 did not help the cause of religious toleration. It is scarcely surprising that Roman Catholics did not achieve full civil liberties until as late as 1829.

Both Bromyard and Upton were centres of Poor Law Unions, established in the 1830s, so each had examples of Victorian institutional architecture in the shape of the dreaded workhouse. Unlike Upton, Bromyard has been able to retain its old workhouse on Bromyard Downs, a discreet distance from the town centre. After the workhouse system was abolished it was adapted first into a hospital and more recently into attractive apartments in a situation that many people living in crowded towns would envy. Here is a good practical example of survival being due to adaptability.

A grammar school was established in Bromyard in the medieval period – another sign of the industry and ambition of its inhabitants. Although this school was replaced by the modern Queen Elizabeth High School, the old grammar school was adapted for use as St Peter's County Primary school. The building is again at a crossroads in its history. Will it survive the adaptability test?

Bromyard has much to offer the visitor. Many come for the gala in July or the folk festival in late September, often camping nearby. This underlines the fact that holidaymakers can use Bromyard as a centre from which to explore nearby countryside such as Bromyard Downs, Bringsty Common or the nature reserve at Ravenshill.

79. Lower Brockhampton Court and gatehouse are delightfully set at the end of a most picturesque drive.

The Malvern Hills and other unspoilt areas are within easy reach by car as are fascinating old houses such as Lower Brockhampton, a moated half-timbered manor house with its own gatehouse, set in idyllic grounds off the A44, a couple of miles outside Bromyard on the way to Worcester.

Historic Herefordshire – the locals still find it hard to accept the unwieldy official name of Hereford and Worcester – also has many glorious old churches, each with its own fascinating history. Try using Bromyard or Ledbury as a base for discovering the delights of old churches at Bosbury, Colwall, Cradley, Mathon – or a dozen others hidden away in the peaceful villages of a county which has managed to remain one of the most rural in England.

Chapter Twelve

Worcester

About eight miles to the north of Malvern lies the cathedral city of Worcester, easily accessible by train, bus or car. Those who come to the Malverns for a holiday might well take a trip into Worcester and would like to know something of what it has to offer, apart from the usual chain-stores that now dominate the high streets of Britain. Like many other towns, Worcester has been spoilt in the 20th century, but retains some attractive features, most of them at the cathedral end of the city. Worcester's Tourist Information Office can supply more details and is to be found in the dignified surroundings of the Guildhall, built in 1721-23 at the cathedral end of the High Street. The magnificent baroque façade of the Guildhall was restored in recent years and inside are various historical displays.

80. Worcester's Guildhall is an architectural gem.

Many visitors arrive in Worcester by train. Alighting at Foregate Street station where the plaque on the railway bridge reminds all who care to look up that they are in the city *semper fidelis in pace et in bello* – ever faithful (to the royalist cause) in peace and war. The final battle of the Civil War took place in the streets of Worcester in 1651 when, Charles I having been executed, his son fought in vain to retain the throne and was forced to flee abroad. In an astonishing reversal of fortunes the leaders of the victorious Parliamentarians eventually begged him to return as monarch in 1660.

Foregate Street derives its name from one of the gates into the town when it was a walled city. The medieval walls have been destroyed, but the City Walls road, whisking traffic along the outskirts of the shopping area, is named in remembrance of the feature demolished by brash planners of a less conservation conscious era.

81. The 19th-century railway bridge over Foregate Street is not in a particularly attractive part of Worcester, but it proclaims the civic pride of ages past. The faithful city has faced numerous struggles since it endured the final battle of the 17th-century Civil War but it still manages to flourish.

The River Severn had a great impact upon the development of Worcester, because of both the river traffic carrying all kinds of goods and the bridge offering one of the few opportunities to cross the massive 'king's high stream of Severn'. The present bridge dates from 1781 though it has been modified from time to time and in recent years, to the enormous relief of local commuters, the huge road traffic burden has been shared with a new bridge which enables traffic to bypass the city altogether. In medieval times one commodity which passed regularly through Worcester was the vital salt from Droitwich – it is a pity that 19th-century city fathers decided to change the old name of Salt Lane to Castle Street. This foolish change was particularly confusing since Worcester's medieval castle was at the other end of town, between King's School and the Severn. The name of Castle Street appears to have been bestowed for no better reason than that the new county gaol, erected at the point where the road bends round to run parallel with the river, sported castellations and other castle-like embellishments.

From medieval times Worcester was very prosperous, and in the 16th century the chronicler Leland remarked upon its wealth which 'standithe most by draping, and noe towne of England at this present tyme maketh so many cloathes yearly as this towne doth'. In fact clothmaking was not Worcester's only industry – leather workers, tilers, glovers and many other craftsmen made substantial contributions to the city's prosperity. In Deansway stands the so-called 'Glover's Needle', reminiscent of the important medieval trade: it is in fact the beautiful perpendicular spire of the old church of St Andrew. The all-pervading power of the Church necessitated dividing the large population of Worcester into numerous parishes in order to ensure adequate provision for their spiritual welfare. Some of the old parish churches have become redundant in the more materialistic modern age, and one of them, St Helen's in the High Street, has been adapted for use as part of the County Record Office.

The cathedral is, of course, the grandest of the ecclesiastical buildings though it has naturally lost some of its medieval glory and the maintenance of its stonework is a constant drain on limited resources. It was once not only the heart of the religious life of the diocese but also the home of the monastic community which was dispersed by Henry VIII. Some of the monastic buildings are still in existence and, notwithstanding their use by the (well-behaved!) pupils of the King's School, the cloisters are a haven of peace. King John's tomb is worth seeing. Valentine Green, Worcester's 18th-century historian, has much to say on this subject, explaining how the king was laid to rest in the lady chapel between the sepulchres of two saints – Oswald and Wulstan, both former bishops of Worcester. In the 16th century a new tomb was prepared for his remains and his effigy was laid upon it, but in the late 18th century there was speculation whether the king's body had been moved to the new tomb or left in the lady chapel! Valentine Green and others urged that there was only one way to find out the truth – and so, one day in July 1797, 'thousands of spectators' viewed the body, covered with 'a vast quantity of the dry skins of maggots', safely reposing in its stone coffin on the floor of the choir. Unfortunately 'the impatience of the multitude' became 'so ungovernable as to

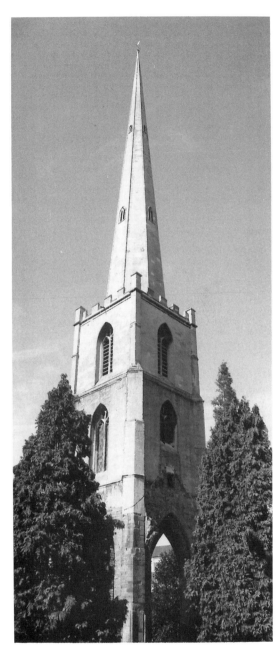

82. Nathaniel Wilkinson's elegant 1751 spire of the now demolished church of St Andrew. Its nickname, 'the glover's needle', recalls one of Worcester's most important trades.

make it necessary to close up the object of their curiosity so precipitantly as to render it extremely difficult to obtain that regular account of a discovery so truly interesting demanded'.One of the king's thumb-bones was removed and is now kept in the cathedral library, not normally open to the public, above the south aisle and overlooking the cloister. The 15-year-old Prince Arthur, son of Henry VII and elder brother of Henry VIII, is also buried in Worcester Cathedral, his simple granite tomb inside a magnificent chantry chapel to the south of the high altar.

Every three years Worcester Cathedral plays host to the Three Choirs Festival, taking it in turns with Gloucester and Hereford. The festivals began informally in the early 18th century, and focused on the music of the cathedrals. Concerts of sacred and secular music were presented in the summer. In 1724, Dr. Thomas Bisse, brother of the Bishop of Hereford, suggested that at the concerts collections should be taken for the benefit of the widows and orphans of poor clergy in the three dioceses, the first such collection being made in Gloucester that year. As time went on the local musicians were joined by nationally recognised performers, who naturally charged fees for their participation. In 1788 George III raised the social status of the festival by visiting it at Worcester, staying with Bishop Hurd at both his palaces – first in Hartlebury and then just a few steps away from the cathedral, across College Yard, at the mellow stone palace in Worcester's Deansway. Hartlebury, some 10 miles north of Worcester, now houses the county museum with many interesting exhibits, particularly of social life.

In these years the works of Handel figured prominently, hence the cathedral's Handel organ. The tradition of annual festivals was maintained throughout the 19th century, though in 1875 they were threatened by the refusal of the dean and chapter of Worcester to allow use of the cathedral, a place of worship, for performances by professional musicians, who were paid to produce secular as well as sacred works. The limited programme which resulted from this decision provoked criticism and mock obituaries, which proved to be premature. The storm subsided and the festivals continued with most of their earlier ingredients. Elgar's music first appeared in the late 19th-century festivals, his *Dream of Gerontius* of which he commented 'This is the best of me', eventually becoming a set piece. He himself conducted this setting of the poem written in 1866 by Cardinal Newman at more than a dozen festivals. The last time he did so was at Hereford in 1933, a few months before his death. Worcester commemorated its famous musician with the 'Gerontius' window in the cathedral.

Pilgrims of a different kind flock to Worcester to see the Royal Worcester Porcelain works, established a few years after the Three Choirs Festival became organised. Formed in 1751, the company was much strengthened by the efforts of Dr. John Wall, whose many ventures included the analysis of Malvern water and the popularising of its use for a variety of medical conditions. Wall died in 1776 and some years later the factory was bought by Thomas Flight, who took Martin Barr into partnership. By this time the royal seal of approval had been given – when George III came to Worcester with Queen Charlotte for the Three Choirs Festival in 1788, they visited the factory, left 10 guineas for the employees and permitted the coveted phrase 'Manufacturers to their Majesties' to be used by the company.

Another famous visitor was Michael Faraday who found Mr. Barr's hospitality rather too much: he could not get to bed until midnight and had to be up at 5 a.m. to catch the London coach. Fortunes flagged somewhat in the middle of the 19th century but were revived, Worcester porcelain now being highly prized for the quality of its design and craftsmanship. For much of the first half of the 20th century Charles Dyson Perrins was chairman of the company. His marvellous collection of Worcester porcelain, with other additions, is on view in the Dyson Perrins Museum adjacent to the factory and within easy walking distance of the cathedral. This museum is fascinating, not just to those who are specialists in china, but to all who enjoy looking at beautiful things. The wide variety of items on display is also illustrative of different aspects of social history – the sumptuous dinner services made for royal families throughout the world, the more homely ware affordable by the less exalted or the special pieces to commemorate political or sporting highlights, all have a place in the museum.

Not far from the cathedral and the Royal Worcester factory is the Commandery, housing a Civil War Centre with audio-visual displays, attractive gardens and tea-room. Troops were quartered here in 1651; after the Battle of Worcester the wounded were carried into this still beautifully preserved 16th-century building, which was for many years the premises of a publishing company. Its new accessibility to the public affords considerable interest. Another interesting place to spend an hour or two is Friar Street, which contains a number of unusual shops and buildings. The Tudor House Museum has exhibits on the domestic and agricultural life

83. The Commandery at Worcester.

84. The quiet courtyard of the concert hall which occupies the refurbished chapel of the Countess of Huntingdon's Connexion.

of the last 400 years. Nearly opposite, the National Trust now has responsibility for the lovely medieval timber-framed house known as Greyfriars.

In Deansway, opposite the old spire of St Andrew's church is the recently restored Countess of Huntingdon's Hall, where a varied programme offers the chance to enjoy simultaneously a concert and the unexpectedly exuberant features of a building originally designed as a nonconformist chapel. John Betjeman described it as a Georgian gem: it served as a chapel for over 200 years from 1773 until 1976, but was threatened with demolition when its dwindling congregation was unable to raise the money needed to prevent its gradual but apparently inevitable decay. However, against all odds, an enthusiastic and determined group set about raising nearly one million pounds to repair the unique building, their efforts now continuing in order to improve the facilities of one of the most extraordinary concert halls in the country.

In this national context, many people would claim that Worcestershire County Cricket Club has the loveliest ground in the country. Admission from the 'New' Road which leads towards the 18th-century bridge sounds very dull, but the reality is that the ground is set against the superb backcloth of the cathedral, with the River Severn running alongside – or, after heavy rain, over – the ground.

For some people it will be enough simply to enjoy the peace of a riverside walk in Worcester, but the city still has a good deal more to offer despite the best efforts of philistine developers who deprived the 'faithful city' of much of its heritage. Medieval markets and fairs have been replaced by modern equivalents. For example,

85. A few minutes' walk from the bustling centre of Worcester is a timeless view up the Severn.

86.   Reindeer Court is a pleasant arcade of modern shop units based on the carefully preserved features of the
15th-century *Reindeer Inn*. It is Worcester's imaginative response to accusations that too much of its historic
past had been bulldozed into a standard and boring town centre.

the Shambles, where once the butchers slaughtered and sold their animals, is now
lined with decidedly more hygienic shops and historic places like Blackfriars and
Deansway have had to make way for modern development such as Crowngate.
There are certain advantages in modern living – and the area around Worcester and
the Malverns has retained many attractive features from the past, commendably
managing to marry them, usually happily, with the benefits of the 20th century.

Bibliography

Allies, Jabez, *Antiquities and Folklore of Worcestershire*, 1852
Baird, Alice, *I Was There*, 1956
Barnes, Gordon, *Frederick Preedy*, 1984
Benedict, St, *Rule*
Berridge, Elizabeth, *The Barretts at Hope End*, 1974
Brown, H. and Bowles, M., *St Matthias at the Link*, 1946
Bulman, Joan, *Jenny Lind*, 1956
Card, the Rev. Henry, *Antiquities of the Priory of Great Malvern*
Cartwright, Bob and Weaver, Cora, *The Elgar Trail*, audio tape, 1991
Chambers, John, *History of Malvern*, 1817
Chambers, John, *History of Worcester*
Community of the Holy Name, *History 1865 to 1950*
Craze, Michael, *King's School, Worcester*, 1972
Dacey, Richard, *History of Organs at Malvern Priory*, 1954
Drake, Daphne, *The Story of Malvern Link*, 1982
Edminson, Vera, *Ancient Misericords in the Priory Church*, 1954
Gaunt, H. C. A., *Two Exiles*, 1946
Gaut, R. C., *History of Worcestershire Agriculture*, 1939
Gray, Edward F., *St Mary's Parish Church, Ripple*
Green, Valentine, *History of Worcester 1796-7*
Grindrod, C., *The Legend of the Ragged Stone*, 1899
Grindrod, R. B., *Malvern Past and Present*, 1865
Hadfield, Alice Mary, *The Chartist Land Company*, 1970
Hall-Jones, Roger, *Jenny Lind*, 1987
Hamand, L. A., *The Ancient Windows of Great Malvern Priory Church*, 1947
Hillaby, Joe, *Book of Ledbury*, 1982
Hurle, Pamela, *Beneath the Malvern Hills*, 1973
Hurle, Pamela, *Bygone Malvern*, 1989
Hurle, Pamela, *Hanley Castle, Heart of Malvern Chase*, 1978
Hurle, Pamela, *The Malvern Hills*, 1984
Hurle, Pamela and Winsor, John, *Portrait of Malvern*, 1985
Hurle, Pamela, *Upton, Portrait of a Severnside Town*, 1979
Lane, R. J., *Life at the Water Cure*, 1846
Langland, William, *Piers the Plowman*
Lawson, Emily, *The Nation in the Parish*, 1884
Lees, Edwin, *The Forest and Chace of Malvern*, 1877
Leisure Hour Journal, 1856 and 1862
Lines, H. H., *The Ancient Camps on the Malvern Hills*, *c*.1897

Lucas, J. W., *Malvern Public Library*, 1940
McMenemey, W. H., *History of Worcester Royal Infirmary*, 1947 *Malvern Advertiser*
Malvern Festival programmes, 1929-39; 1977-91
Malvern Gazette
Malvern News
The Map Shop, Upton, *The Malvern Hills*, set of three maps, 1984
Moody, Catherine, *Silhouette of Malvern*, 1953
Moore, Jerrold Northrop, *Edward Elgar: A Creative Life*, 1984
Moore, Jerrold Northrop, *Spirit of England*, 1984
Morris, C. (ed.), *The Journeys of Celia Fiennes*
Nash, T. R., *Collections for a History of Worcestershire*, 1799
Noake, John, *Rambles in Worcestershire*, 1863
Nott, James, *The Church and Monastery of Moche Malverne*, 1885
Oddfish, J. B., *Malvern Punch*, 1865
Postle, David, *A Glimpse of Old Ledbury*, 1988
Ransome, Mary (ed.), *Bishop Hurd's Survey of Diocese*, 1968
A Restored Invalid, *The Metropolis of the Water Cure*, 1858
Robinson, S. F. Gavin, *History of St Michael & All Angels, Ledbury*, 1975
Rowe, A. P., *One Story of Radar*, 1948
Salt Brassington, W., *Historic Worcestershire*, 1894
Savage, George, *The Story of Royal Worcester*, 1973
Smith, Brian, *History of Malvern*, 1978
Southall, Mary, *Description of Malvern*, 1823
Stanford, S. C., *The Malvern Hill Forts*, 1973
Stroller, A., Various articles in local press, 1930s
Sutton, A., *Malvernia, the First Santler Motor Car*, 1987
Three Counties Agricultural Society Show catalogues
Tilleys, *Guide to Ledbury*
Tomos, Dafydd, *Michael Faraday in Wales*
Turberville, T. C., *19th Century Worcestershire*, 1852
Waite, Vincent, *Malvern Country*, 1979
Walker, J. Severn, *Architectural Sketches*, 1863
Waller, Deborah (ed.), *Bromyard: Round and About*, 1991
Weaver, Cora, *The Thirteenth Enigma*, 1990
Weaver, Cora, *Charles Darwin and Evelyn Waugh in Malvern*, 1991
Willis-Bund, J. W. and Page, Wm. (ed.), *Victoria County History, 1901-1926*
Wilson, J. M., *The Worcester Liber Albus*, 1920
Winsor, John, *Malvern Priory*, 1981
Winsor, John, *What to See in Malvern*, 1991

Index

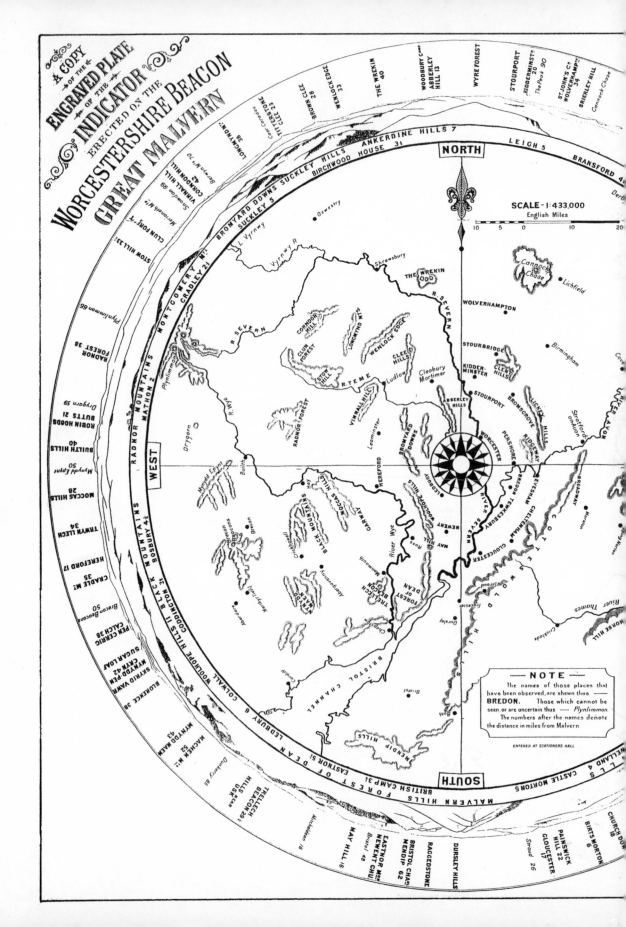